Cumbria
to
Kwai

T. Stewart

National Ex-Services News

First published in 2000 by
National Ex-Services News
98 Charles Street
Stockport SK1 3JT
Tel: 0161 480 0114
Fax: 0161 477 2681
Email: arthurlane@nesanews.freeserve.co.uk

© National Ex-Services News 2000

ISBN 1 897666 04 7

Printed by Juma, 44 Wellington Street, Sheffield S1 4HD

Dedicated to all former servicemen and in particular those who were incarcerated by the Japanese during the Second World War.

The pain and sacrifice were worthy of the final victory over such a despicable enemy.

Tom (Chuck) Stewart

SKYMASTER TOM STEWART

Mr Tom Stewart, the original writer of this column, as then "West Coast Homing, by Skymaster", has died, aged 68. After previously suffering a series of heart attacks over a period of time, Tom died outside his Cleator Moor loft last week, while preparing his birds for the weekend's racing.

Tom, who lived at Todholes Road, leaves a wife, Ruby, and daughter, Valerie, and two grandsons, Stuart and Neil, who, with their father, fly as David Buchanan and Sons, from Whitehaven.

Tom resumed his association with pigeon racing when he was freed from the infamous Changi Camp in 1945 having been a prisoner of war of the Japanese since the fall of Singapore in 1942. He worked on the Burma railway while a prisoner and suffered from malaria, dysentery and beri-beri.

Tom, who had started work on his autobiography, was in his youth a well known footballer and played for the 1st and 2nd Manchester Regiments while in the Army.

He was the author of a book published several years ago, "Cumbria Pigeons", and was also known through featuring on BBC Radio Carlisle's Sunday morning programme, "How Do", talking on pigeon matters. His funeral interment took place yesterday, Wednesday, at St Leonard's Church, Cleator.

Part I

The 'Roaring Twenties' were un-noticed in my little West Cumbria village, where all energies were directed toward providing the next meal for the hungry families. The Hungry Twenties would have been a more apt description. A lot of young men of the village had not marched back from the war and for those that did there was a general bewilderment at the lack of evidence of a great going forward, towards a build up of creating a country fit for heroes to live in. The hero image took a tumble with the cessation of hostilities and although M.M.'s were ten a penny they could not buy clogs for the clogless or shirts for the shirtless. As one poor demented mother declared, "My two kids haven't a clog to their back". This meant the humiliating process of applying to the 'Parish' for a document which had to be taken to 'Johnny Fikki's' to procure the footwear. I know I have knocked on Mr Murray's door on Trumpet Terrace on more than one occasion. If possible, these missions were always undertaken when it was dark and many's the time I have bumped into school mates either entering or leaving Mr Murray's front door, which was situated 'between lamps'. These being strategically placed 80 yards apart on the pavement (or pad) edge. No bus rides in those days, and going from points A to B was best accomplished on 'Shank's Pony', progress being quickened up a bit by walking a lamp and running a lamp. This spartan existence killed off the weak and made greyhounds of the survivors.

Although we were a small community there were recognised splits according to religious beliefs. You were either a 'Prody-dog' or a 'Roman Candle' with the the smattering of Wesleyan or Presbyterian to cause greater confusion.

The Catholic community were the descendants of the general influx of Irish nationals who came to work in the village cotton mill or the iron ore mines, which at that time (1905/1920) were in full production, and even the Forge hammer beat a non-stop tattoo turning out spades and shovels by the hundreds.

The end of the 14/18 war saw the decline of these activities and the gradual run-down commenced with one national crisis after another. This was the era when the rich were very rich and the poor very poor. My own Grandfather was direct from Londonderry as was my Grandmother, but where most were of Catholic beliefs he was a staunch supporter of the 'Billy Boys'. He would get a 'drop of the crater' down him at the weekends and then proclaim to all and sundry "The Stewarts are here, let the battle commence!". There was always plenty to take up the challenge, the village 'Bobby' being grossly outnumbered and deciding that his line of duty lay elsewhere, looking for poachers, being the favourite outlet. This necessary duty took him well out of the line of fire until such times as the warring factions had thumped each other to a standstill. When the dust had settled the 'Bobby' would re-enter the battle zone with not a bloodstain on his medal ribbons and raring to go when all around had decided to call it a day (or night).

Poaching was rife in those days and rabbits were scarce along with hares, pheasants etc. My father had ferrets, which he carried under his shirt next to his skin. Rabbit nets were carried in a jacket 'all round' pocket and to complete the team he had a Lurcher dog called 'Ted', who was the most cunning of animals. This dog was known to hunt, kill and carry home without being prompted by my father. Ted was also a thief and thought a local butcher shop was his larder. This so-called shop was the front parlour of a house on Main Street, being rented by 'Jonty' Simon and only opened on Saturday mornings. I remember a hullabaloo one Saturday, when Ted had sneaked in under the butcher table and fastened his teeth into a sausage which happened to be hanging conveniently over the side. Unfortunately this sausage was just part of a long string of the same items and Ted streaked for home with Jonty in full cry carrying a 'cleaver'. If he hadn't skidded on one of the trailing sausages I imagine that Ted would have been part of the next consignment. As it was the animal managed to escape with a dozen or so and my father managed to retrieve half of them before the hungry dog gulped them down. They finished up in our big frying pan.

Jonty was quite a character and lived on a small holding between Woodend Station and the very active Clintz Quarry. He did all his own slaughtering on the farm and I remember the time when he was accused of shoving sheep over the quarry face and then cutting them up for sale. It wouldn't have been so bad if they had been his own sheep but it was alleged otherwise. A chap called Billy Callagher worked part time for him and poor Gallagher took the blame which landed him in jail. We kids would follow Gallagher on his release chanting:

"Gallagher, Gallagher do not weep,
It was not you that stole the sheep,
Up the Clintz it was seen climbing,
And pulverised by Jonty Simon."

Around about this time there was a mechanical and electrical genius, who was born before his time. A chap called Harry Roberts, who would apply locomotion to practically anything. He managed to set up an 'electric hare' track in a field near the New Hipp, on Jacktrees Road. All the local poachers were invited to compete with their multi-breed lurcher dogs. Not to be outdone my father entered Ted in the 'Moor Handicap'. Ted won through to the semi-finals when calamity struck in the form of a very stormy thunder shower which affected the hare track. When the dogs were released for this heat Ted was away like a bullet after the decoy when all of a sudden the hare stopped and Ted was on it like a shot. When he realised the so-called hare was just a rabbit skin on a frame he took no further part in the proceedings and from that day on would have no part of it. The dog was too intelligent for this sort of caper. One time he managed to get trapped in a rock fall on the Fells and my father and friends were out two nights trying to extricate him. When he was carried home his front left leg was found to be broken. No vet visits in those days but the next best thing was the extremely efficient handling by old Joe Scrugham. He had an improvised splint on Ted in no time and it says much for his tender care that the dog was dashing around nimbly on three legs. He had to be nimble because Jonty was still after him!

Some of the poaching element (and there were many of them) would direct all their skills and energies into evading the 'Beck-watcher' (River Bailiff) by clicking, grappling or snaring salmon, smelt or trout. When the salmon were on the run up stream they had to negotiate a very wide weir down Sandy Bottom, and given the right amount of flood water cascading down the weir they would wriggle up and make stupendous leaps over the top. This was when the poachers would dash along the moss covered stones and attempt to 'click' the fish with a massive barbed hoop which was affixed to the end of a bamboo cane, made more secure with stout twine which ran up the bamboo and looped around the wrist of the hunter. The poachers worked as a team. There were look-outs spaced out along the river banks on the watch for the Beck watcher and his black Labrador dogs. The poor man hadn't a chance of making an arrest and very few of the wily poachers were ever caught.

The great love of my father was pigeon racing, a love which was passed on to me and I still have to this day. My father, who was known far and wide as 'Wee Jimmy', was a wizard at conditioning birds for the racing events, and could win against the odds time and again. Competition was fierce with the likes of Tommy Housby, Johan Jackson, Joe Graham, Tommy Close, Cromwells, the Dawsons, John Tallon, and many more. Friday night was a bustling night in the village when the pigeons were basketted and carried up to Woodend Station, for race marking, rubber ringing and despatched by rail under the supervision of a nominated convoyer. The birds would be liberated on the following day and the pigeon fanciers would be on look-out at their lofts, fantail decoys in hand and hope in their breast. At that time there was a local book-maker called Pat Dunne, who would give the odds against lofts to win, pigeon to win, you name it he would take your bet. There would be a crowd of punters near the allotments where the pigeon lofts were located and if there were two or more pigeons trapping at the same time the punters would start shouting for their particular loft. It was more like a fox hunt at the kill. There was just one hired pigeon clock in the club and this had to be set up near a central point to the lofts and many a race was won or lost on the run-in to the clock. These pigeon fanciers would starve to feed their birds.

The same thing could be said of the whippet men, who could be seen exercising their small fast dogs every day in the week, ready for the weekly handicaps, which took place down the 'Lonny' on the cricket field. These dogs were taught to run 'to the rag' and had to maintain a straight line of running within the confine of the string markers of the individual tracks. Many were the tricks played so as to get a good handicap. There would be the dodge of chewing gum between the toes, or the elastic ring out of a lemonade bottle which was forced tightly over the paws. The intention of these tricks was to slow the animals down so as to get a shorter run for the next heat. The animals were sped on their way by the handler or 'chucker', who held the dogs one hand under the breast and the other under the back legs ready for the starter signal when the animal was thrown forward in a rhythmic fashion, so that the front legs would make a balanced contact with the track. A good 'chucker' was as good as a 5 yard start. If the 'chucker' had been 'got at' it wasn't unknown for him to give the dog's testicles a good nip on the point of release. The yelp of agony was just put down to the excitement of the chase to come, but the ill treatment was very effective in slowing down the poor dog.

Hound Trailing was another popular pastime and if you owned one of these Trail Hounds you could be in clover provided the animal was keen to have a go. It didn't have to be a winner but rather be the middle pawn for the betting money. Dogs could be fixed or nobbled to lose very heavily when the current form would indicate that they should win by a field. Nowadays there are scouts situated at the many blind spots on the trail but not in the 1920's! The trail runner would set off with his aniseed-saturated rag with a spare bottle of the mixture for re-contamination of the trailing rag. The route from the Cleator Sports field would usually be: follow the Lonny Beck down through 'Molly Sharps', cross the Beck at the Forge and up through the 'Neuk' crossing the Fell Road at the gamekeeper's lodge, and straight up the Fells to the Deer Park and across the face of Dent as far as Kitchen's Reservoir, when the homeward run would begin via Ehen Beck, The Flosh, across Jacktrees Road and down the Coach Road skirting the Quarry and dropping down on to the High Line before entering the Sports Field, to the howls and shouts of the owners who were spread out in line behind the rope finishing line. The winner was decided by two judges, one at each end of the finishing line. The Bookies would have been busy whilst the Hounds were on the trail but if the punters weren't 'in the know', it was money thrown away. On the 'blind spots' on the trail, dogs would be lured off with bits of liver or even a bitch 'on heat'. This could cause chaos and anything would win but the favourite wouldn't! This one would be held until the main pack was out of sight. Another trick was to slip the dog a feed laced with plenty of salt immediately before the 'off'. This had to be done discreetly and unseen. There were many interpretations of what constituted a good hound and there were no laid down rules. Two of the more successful Hounds that I recall were 'Mountain' and sometime later 'McDuff'. Both these animals were reputed to be Foxhound/Cur Dog cross, the Cur Dog being the ordinary farmer's sheep dog. The Foxhound would provide the stamina and trailing instinct and the Cur Dog the speed and cunning. This sport is still very strong in the Cleator Moor area.

A noted character in the village was one Hughie Morgan, a real Irish National, who wasn't afraid to announce that he was a past member of the I.R.A. and had fought for the 'Ballicuddlio Brigade' against the Black and Tans: "Sure, its codding me yez are?" says old Barney Lynch giving himself a kick at his own ignorance. "Niver the Divil" says Hughie, "I'll be afther taking on any man who conterdicts me cockerosity so don't you'se adapt that altitude wit me".

Barney backs off in confusion and then attempts to butter Hughie up. "I've got the price in me pocket, Hughie, will you'se do me the honour?". "That I will", says Hughie, "Just so long as we go to the 'Cellar', it's a good drop of 'Porter' there and the Sacred Heart is hanging behind the Bar". Off they go down the Brow only to find the doors are still shut but admittance was gained by finding the hole in the sandstone and kicking into the aperture with the 'duck-neb' clogs. This brought the landlord around from the house and into the bar..

"Yez are late", says Barney. "Aye I am an all", says Arthur adding that he had more than his share the night before.

"Well, pull me a dacent pint of Porter, I've got a throat-full of feathers" chimed in Hughie.

The crack got round to the 'ould country' and various topics of nature, it being spring at this time. There were various outrageous tales of the unexpected to the normal or natural behaviours. Barney reckoned that it didn't always mean that a straw carrying bird was en route to a nestmaking operation, as he had witnessed a starling sitting on a building and picking its 'tathe' with the straw. To which Hughie told the tale of the pup which was being trained to correct behaviour in the house. For two days the pup had been subjected to the indignity of having its nose rubbed in it before being thrown out of the house. The owner came home one day to see the pup doing its business, rubbing its nose in the mess and throwing itself out of the door! He reckoned that the training was incomplete and was considering extending the training to playing dominoes. Before the money and slating facilities ran out the whole gamut of animal and bird behaviour had been covered, there were rabbits which worried dogs, a 'Banty' which won a pigeon race, and a cat which had swam across from the Isle of Man without a rudder..

There was also a race horse entered for a race and being heavy in foal at the time. In fact, it actually stopped half way through the race and gave birth to the foal before going on to win. The foal - according to Barney - was second. When Hughie was full of the lotion he would climb onto the back yard coal sheds on Prospect and inform the whole village that he would "fly tonight to the Mountains of Mourne". No parachute - no flying kite just a straight off free fall!

He never gave up the idea that one night he would successfully take off and land in the 'ould country'. When he eventually died at a ripe old age my father and Uncle Bill Rooney were asked to carry him down the narrow winding stairs so that he could be 'coffinned' and prepared for the 'wake'. One took the shoulders whilst the other backed down the stairs. Everything went well until Uncle Bill dropped the shoulders on to the stairs whereupon the wind left the body with a loud whoosh! The two carriers were petrified, but not for long! There was a leap from the top of the stairs and a general mix up of live and dead bodies before the mad scramble for the open door. They never stopped running until they got as far as Gutterby, thinking Hughie had come alive again and was hotly in pursuit!

The aftermath of the First World War threw up a multitude of characters who travelled around the villages to try and eke out a living one way or another. There were singing troubadors, the 'Tin Whistle' man, 'Taffy Dan', 'Leather Lugs' - all with their own individual characteristics. Some of the singers could compete with anything on the 'box' these days, and some would make your ear ache or scatter the cats in all directions. The 'Tin Whistle' man would go through the same repertoire, his mackintosh tattered and torn, swinging in the breeze whilst he did a jig cheered on by a motley crowd of village urchins. If he got no money for his efforts he always got a mug of tea and some bread and cheese. I think he was happy with that. 'Taffy Dan' had a different approach being the owner of a flea bitten nag and a flat cart. He would stand on the cart and sound a bugle call, the bugle hung around his neck in proper military fashion. The bugle call sounded just like TAFFY

DAY! TAFFY DAN! TAFFY DAN! - hence the name. He dealt in rags and jam jars, for which he paid out in balloons for the kiddies. It was a common expression in those days to tell some one to 'pull yourself together, Taffy Dan's coming'. This when the britches arse was flying in the breeze - as it often was.

'Leather Lugs' was a character to be avoided as he was very unpredictable and being armed with a hefty stick it was the sensible thing to keep at a distance. If he received no rabbit skins or rags on his rounds he would go into a tirade of cursing to the effect that we had "Robbed his Mother and killed his Father" and every one was either a 'whore', a 'bugger' or a 'bastard'! During the summer time the donkey man would pay an occasional visit to the village. The charge per trot being ¹/2d was beyond the financial reach of 'us lot' but nevertheless provided us with endless fun in other ways. The donkeys would be walked or trotted down the back street and round the corner for another 50 yards before turning back. After a couple of runs they would be sent off on their own with the small rider clinging to the mane or the lug. Once the animals turned the corner the scruff lot from Prospect would take over and the donkeys would be forced into a gallop. They soon became the fastest running donkeys in the West. One time we changed our tactics and decided to carry out a rustling operation by hustling the bewildered beasts into old Mrs Dawson's back yard on the backside of Church 'Went'. There were six donkeys in the yard at one time. The riders having been pulled off and chased in another direction. The yard door was locked on the inside and we made our escape by climbing over into the next yard thereby creating the greatest disappearing act ever. It was a full hour before the poor demented donkey man found the animals when one of them decided to bray, by which time Mrs Dawson had enough manure to plant a few stones of potatoes. One would have thought that she would have been delighted at this bonus but not so! From that day we daren't retrieve our ball from her yard and we were automatically put on the black list.

The policeman at that time was one Jack Mellor who could be guaranteed to stop you in your tracks with a swish of the cape or a clip around the earhole with the gloves. The mere sight of him would awaken the instincts into looking for an escape route because to Jack everyone was guilty until proven innocent. These were the accepted police tactics of those days and it effectively cut out the need for juvenile courts and also formulated a healthy respect for the law and for your 'betters'. School teachers, Vicars, Priests and School Governors came into this category and warranted a lift of the cap or a pull of the fore-lock. Unless you had been on the receiving end of one of Miles Bawden '2d all offs' (tuppenny) in which case the fore finger to the head would suffice.

One day during a very warm summer in the 20's a lot of we lads were convorting the 'Beck' at a place known as Sandy Bottom. This was just one of the many swimming areas on this stretch of the water, others being the 'Mill', the 'Steps' or the 'Dub' and if you couldn't swim by the age of 7 years old you would be classified as a lassie-lad. However, we were 'dogpaddling' under-water and doing submarine techniques and generally enjoying ourselves in the 'Nuddie' on this par-ticular day, when Jack Mellor made a one man attach from the flank. Panic all round with no time to dress but just enough to grab the pile of clothing, usually just a pair of corduroy shorts, shirt and clogs. Jack was swinging the stick in all directions and herding the twenty or so naked lads up into the main street of the village. This was the first case of col-lective streaking ever known and the village lasses were cross-eyed try-ing to keep us all in the picture, even when we scattered in all directions to the safety of our own back-yards. The village lock-up window was broken that evening and so well organised that it was assumed that some being from outer space had done the foul deed. Knock for knock seemed fair enough to me. Jack was an ex-Navy P.T. instructor and could often be seen dashing down Church Went and out into the open country via the Lonny. He always wore a big white sweater for these jaunts and usually carried out this activity after dark, so much so that courting couples were panic stricken time and again to see this large white figure ghosting along in his 'sand-shoes'. Of the many things that could be said of Jack Mellor no one could accuse him of not carrying out his duties with zeal and ability and possibly a few more like him at the present time could keep the 'yobo' types in line.

There were many characters in this village in my school days and their different ways of speech and behaviours was a constant source of amusement to the rest of the inhabitants. There was Jimmy Foy of the big black beard and the finest fish line caster in the land. He could 'Fly cast' on a bed of daisies and nominate his next catch. There was Benny McCourt who could be depended upon to say the wrong thing at the wrong time on most or every occasion. He answered the door one day to a 'door to door salesman'. This chap was really putting the spiel across, especially when he realised Benny was an R.C. and could possibly be interested in holy books. "I have some lovely books here, Sir. Prayer Books, Hymn Books or the more sophisticated type. For instance, sir, have you the 'Life of Christ' in the house?". "The life of Christ, ye say?, Sure, I haven't the life of a bloody dog", says Benny. Exit salesman with all his lines intact. Another time Benny attended the funeral of a friend and at the time of sprinkling soil on the coffin, he said "Well yez have been a grand mate of mine for a long time and if God spares me it won't be long till I'm with ye". He was once sent to a local mine by the Labour Exchange who considered eight years on the dole was a tidy stretch and a job of work would relieve the monotony for him.

The iron ore tubs were filled at the face and then pushed or 'trailed' to the lift up point at the shaft bottom. Benny didn't think there was any future in this occupation for him and when the pit manager asked if he done any 'trailing', Benny replied: "Sure and didn't I trail the wife and tree kids all the way from Ireland".

The mile walk to the pit had exhausted Benny and the unaccustomed exercise had aged him, that and the fear of being taken on, so much so that the mine manager advised him to go home and sleep it off. "That I will" says Benny. "Let me see, it's Tuesday now so I'll ask the wife to wake me on Friday .

We often had concerts in the 'Jubilee Rooms' down Church Went and the same artists were called upon every time and each did exactly the same act, sang the same song or mucked up the same magic trick on each occasion. They were all repeat shows with very little variation. One variation really brought the house down when Sammy Morton appeared on stage with his well known talking doll - Fred. Now Fred was good and it always appeared that Fred was in charge,whether by accident or design is open to conjecture. Fred's mouth was always shut but Sammy's mouth could be seen to utter every syllable and making the veins stand out on his neck with the effort. On this particular night Fred was supposed to be going through the "Alphaget" when a leg broke on the three-legged stool and Charlie's false teeth shot out at the same time. It was a hilarious moment and there were shouts of 'core' encore' Sammy (or Fred) refused to perform again that night.

14

Another chap would render the same Lord's Prayer tune time after time and render is the operative word. He didn't sing it so much as run it down and the noise was excruciating to the ears. The lads would bend down under the seats and make howling dog noises whilst he was 'rendering'. I think those noise accompaniments gave a bit of class to the noises from the stage. He was also a false start man and if he had been a racehorse would have been disqualified (or shot) every time.

Another character which springs to mind was one 'Half Hung Tom'. Apparently Tom's dog had been worrying chickens, and this lack of animal control was considered to be a heinous crime, the punishment for which was 'transporting' to the Penal Colony (Australia). Tom got himself so worked up that he decided to hang himself, but fortunately for him the rope broke so it just constituted a 50% hanging. Hence the name - Half Hung Tom.

There was also Johnny 'Cinder-Heels' who methodically placed one foot in front of the other as if his clogs were full of cinders. Another was 'Empty-Clogs', who could be heard clopping along in the duck-neb clogs for miles. They appeared to be three sizes too big for him and sounded hollow.

The months were broken up by various seasons of play. There would be the spinning top season, the marble season, the hoop, the stalls (where it was a pin, button or marble a go). There was peggi-stick and 'duck 'n alley' and many more ancient games which had their beginning centuries before. The spinning tops which had to be kept on the move with the whip and lash was the cause of many a broken window, and it was the accepted policy to flee the scene as quickly as possible. Nothing so sissy as standing ground and admitting responsibility. This game had to be played on the Main Street where there was a lot of horse muck. There was little fear from cars in those days but of the very few that did appear one was to hit me for six whilst I was playing 'mad horses'. I had the ropes tied to my upper arms to represent the reins whilst my playmate was the driver running behind this mad horse which was high stepping, taking 'titch' and all the other antics when this car came flying along at 15 m.p.h. and scooped me up in its path. I can't remember much about the accident, but can remember the mummy-like bandages which were part of me for quite some time and ended my mad horse career. There was quite a variation of marble games, ringie, lag or folly toe (lovely names) and even an indoor variation for wet days when you could pull out the proddy mat to one side and bang the marbles against the wall. The idea being to try and rebound to the same point as your opponent's previously rebound one. If you could span the two marbles with the little finger and thumb of the right hand, the opponent's marble became yours. This game was known as 'spanney' (another lovely name).

The mention of proddy mats reminds me that my family nearly always had one on the frame and homing from school meant bread and jam (limited), followed by a marked out portion of the mat to complete before being allowed out to play until bed time, which was 6.30 p.m. in winter time and 7.00 p.m. in summer. Try tearing a kiddie away from the Tele at that time today and the cruelty inspector would move in on you. Most Saturday mornings were a 7.00 a.m. rise and away to the 'Cinder bank' to pick a hessian sack full of cinders or coal chippings which had been drawn from the fire holes under the steam boilers, at the Iron Ore Pit Head. This had to be humped the two miles along the old railway siding and then down the 'Brist' (breast), this being some sloping fields running down past the Vicarage and then up the 'Lonney' to the village.

The two village schools were divided by a 5 foot wall and no-one would dare to go over into enemy territory to retrieve a ball. Except for the occasional stone fight the two factions got on fairly well. Individual fights were conducted in a gentlemanly fashion. First of all would be the challenge, i.e. confront the intended opponent, give a light tap on the right side of the chest followed by one on the left side of the chest and then a light slap on the cheek at the same time chanting "There's your buff, there's your blow, there's your one to start with, one, two, three, I am the master of thee!". If the challenge was taken up the fight would commence there and then or at a place to be designated after school. This procedure was no doubt a flash back to the middle ages, duel preliminaries. There were many explosive situations when fights would break out there and then but at no time would the boot or clog be used. Any one using the feet in these feuds would be labelled 'lassie-lad' and be cut down to size by the spectators. Alas, the opposite would apply these days.

The teachers were very strict, but on the whole - just. I can only remember one exception and he was hated by all the lads. He came to school on a bike but didn't always ride it home. He could never be sure whether the two wheels would still be affixed to the machine or whether the wind would still be in the tubes. The more he lambasted us the more his bike got the treatment. Discipline we would accept but out and out bullying tactics such as his were not on. He didn't use the cane but had a small wooden bat which was wielded in a vicious smack across the posterior whilst the victim was touching his toes. In all fairness it must be said that the Headmaster didn't know about this weapon and we weren't prepared to 'clat', but to deal with it in our own way. One day this bat was pinched and some sharp nails were knocked through to the impact surface, the protrusion being about $1/8$". Some of the class knew about this modification and this knowledge gave us the incentive to be good as gold even though this teacher was cruising up and down like a shark. Eventually, one of the lads had to make the wrong move which meant the touch the toes position ready for the under arm smash. The teacher brought the bat out from its hiding place and brought it across the buttocks of the victim. This lad let out a frenzied howl and took off for the classroom door like a greyhound out of the trap. The bat was still sticking to his backside, when he shot through the great hall past the astonished Headmaster, who was sat at his high desk on the dais, like a king on the throne. The bat was dislodged as the poor lad hit the second pair of swing doors and all was revealed to the Head. It was the day of reckoning for this little tyrant of a teacher. The Head dealt with him first and then for an irate parent to barge into the school demanding revenge. A month later he was transferred to another area and we later heard was a model teacher. The lesson was learnt.

School days were to end all too soon and even though I had qualified for Secondary School education the decision was made that I leave school at 14 and be hired out to a farm in the middle of nowhere. The winter of '28 was continual frost and snow when I took my first step into the outside world. The wage was £2 for the remaining three months of the term plus my keep. For this three shillings and four pence per week I had to do the normal farm chores plus the added slavery of helping the 'Missus'. The farmer himself was a jovial character but the Missus was a vinegary tyrant with a sadistic nature. For instance she told me to enter this small building to bring something to the house knowing full well that a dog in there had a vicious nature. Quite naturally this animal had a go at me and fastened its teeth in my thigh before I could move out of the way. The boss dashed in and kicked the dog to one side but I was badly bitten by now. The Missus made the excuse that Jack (the dog) had to get acquainted with me some time and now was as good a time as any. The boss really gave her a dressing down and this mollified me a little, but Jack and I were sworn enemies from that day on. This woman had me turning the handle of both the butter churn and the milk separator at one and the same time and this was not an easy task, when it is considered that the turning speeds of these machines were different. The concentration brought on a head-ache. If she had only realised I could have been brushing up at the same time if the brush had been stuck between my teeth (or elsewhere for that matter). A lot of these characteristic failings could have been forgiven if she had been some sort of cook but she had no affinity with the culinary arts whatever. Breakfast consisted of gruel porridge slopped into a basin which had to be drank rather than scooped. The tea was then poured into the same basin and one spoonful of sugar doled out for each person. There was usually home cured bacon and a frizzled egg with one slice of bread each. The table manners were atrocious and it developed into a race of guzzling down and vacating the table before the boss had finished because when he moved everybody moved. We weren't so much people as Hound-dogs. The midday meal was the same routine of a shovelling on of potatoes, veg. and very little meat followed by watery rice pudding on the same plate. There was quite an economy on the washing up side.

My household chores were to come to an abrupt but thankful end in this way. It was a wash day and I was pumping away with the 'poss stick on the clothes in the 'dolly tub' when the missus came bustling in with garbled instructions to put the clothes in the boiler when the water had come to a boil. To me clothes are clothes with no distinction between woollens, linens or coloureds so that when the bit 'set pot' started on the boil, I collected all the clothes which were lying in three separate little piles and bunged them all in the boiling water. Some time afterwards the missus came into the wash house and demanded to know where the clothes were. "In the boiler" said I. "What!!!" she shrieked before grabbing the big boiler stick to fish out the articles. The first item was, or had been, a sock but was now a yard long, the same with most of the items. The bed sheets were multi-coloured and the coloureds were - well - coloured! I thought the woman had run amok when she attacked me with the big boiler stick. I parried, the first strike with the poss-stick before deciding to make a hasty retreat but unfortunately the house cat had the same idea. Both the cat and I reached the door at the same time with the missus in full cry. The stupid cat got between my feet and sent me into a forward roll on the cobbled yard, thereby saving my life because as I tripped forward, the blow which was intended for my head just glanced off my shoulder. The momentum of the fall brought me right up on to my feet and quickly out of the danger zone. The boss had been a witness to this skirmish and was holding his sides bellowing with laughter. That was before he saw his long socks and the still longer, 'Long John's'!

From that day on I was banished from the house which delighted me greatly even though I was given the most menial of tasks like cleaning out the pigsties, clearing the dry closet and tidying the midden.

I was an eager beaver for work but wanted to be involved in the more important tasks like milking (by hand), snagging turnips and the very pinnacle of farm service (to me) of sitting on the front of a 'block' cart and driving the horse. The first day I asked the boss permission to have a go at the milking, he indicated that I start at the top stall away from the light of the door. It was difficult to make out anything other than the outline of animals standing in their separate stalls, and being an obedient sort of lad I plonked my milking stool (or copy) down beside this big outline, sat on the stool, placed the bucket between the knees in the approved manner and prepared to extract the milk. Anyone watching would have been forgiven for thinking that I was a famous concert pianist setting out his stalls to give forth with a Strauss Waltz. I reached out to commence and something told me I was on the wrong end of a bad joke, the 'something' being the hind legs of a very indignant bull! I bounced off the back wall of the byre before 'high-tailing' it for the safety of the great outside. I considered the farmer had manipulated the position to administer the great 'touche' in retaliation for his long socks and 'longer' long Johns! I just took it and said nowt. A feeling of neutrality existed from that day until the day I walked out of the farm yard at the end of term but not before giving Jack (the dog) a kick up the arse. It had greeted me on arrival and I said goodbye on departure in the same vein. Justice had been done.

Hello And Goodbye

I distinctly remember counting the £2 over and over again and evaluating it against 1 dog bite, 1 kick from the larger than life bull, 3 cracks with the boiler stick and three months hard labour in the hardest winter for half a century. This vast fortune was handed over to my old Grandma who rewarded me with half a crown pocket money to do for my term end week off. The other had to be used to get me kitted out for my next 6 monthly hiring.

The hirings were more like a cattle market with farm labourers standing in little groups and farmers standing a little way off, assessing the likeliest lads, who apparently had to have faultless fetlocks, withers and hocks, before the big decision being made to hire for 6 months. The usual questions were asked as to the candidates capabilities, previous experience etc. "Is thoo for hire?" was the starter and always finished with a haggle over the money required for the 6 monthly contract. "A'hll gie thee £6 and thoo can sleep with't lass" was one of the corny jokes which had been passed on for years, followed by "Can t' milk and ploo, hes' t' done any dyking?". So the inquisition went on and on before the final decision was made. Then followed the ritual of the shilling in the hand which was supposed to be the binding of the contract which entitled the farmer to call on you any time day or night. Rates of pay were usually £4 first time with a £2 increase every six months, if you stopped on the same farm. This was subject to negotiation and satisfaction to both parties. Some farmers would throw in free washing but most would leave this problem to the poor old farm labourer.

Tommy Shops

Word quickly got round if a farm had the reputation for being a bad 'tommy-shop' (poor cuisine) or the farmer was too much of a slave driver. Some of the stories told by the farm labourers were incredible to the point of disbelief. One lad told the story of a farm where the farmer instructed him to put plenty of muck in the tatie stitches because taties were "gay hungry" items which required plenty of muck. Dinner time that day was 'tatie-pot' and when the labourer examined his doled up dinner said to the farmer "By God, thoo's right, Boss, taties are hungry

The author, Tom Stewart

They're
off!

Nearly
home!

Last
gasp!

22

Cleator Football Club, 1924

Cleator Junior Fell Runners

My Dad, Wee Jimmy and Wilson Pied Hen,
winner three years on the trot, Swindon

A few whippet men on the 'Moor', 1926

Montreal Street, Cleator, 1910

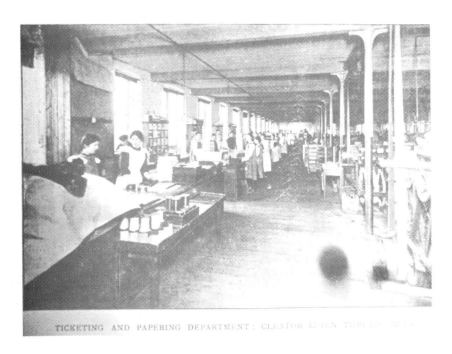

TICKETING AND PAPERING DEPARTMENT: CLEATOR LINEN THREAD MILLS

Cleator Mill football team, 1918

26

Cleator Pigeon Fanciers Club

Tom and pals' racing club

Old Police Cells,
Cleator

'The Cellar', Cleator

things". "Hoo's that me lad?" said the unsuspecting farmer. "Well", said the farm lad, "They've het all me meat"! Another lad, still on the tatie-pot said that this dish was a one-sided effort at his place of work. All the meat was put in at the farmer's end of the huge dish. There was chaos one day when one of the farm labourers saw his chance to turn the dish round before the commencement of the meal. When the missus started dishing it out the boss first, and then in order of priority, the poor old farmer could only glare, thinking the wife had put it on the table the wrong way round!

Another farm had three farm hands as well as the two big strapping farmer's sons and it was a well known fact that when the missus shouted the meal was ready it was imperative that no-one slipped or there was nothing left. It was said that the 'nipper' (the youngest labourer) had died of malnutrition after being given the elbow by the bigger lads too often. Talk about feet in the trough!!

Wet days provided something of a problem for ensuring that the labour was still gainfully employed. The usual job would be threshing but where this wasn't possible it had been known for the farmer to instruct the labourer to "Shove'd dog in t' stable, shut door, then it won't get oot in t'rain, then put a bag roond thee shoulders and brush t' yard up and tidy t' midden". En route to work in the fields the labourer would be instructed "Bash on", "A'll shut guats, piss walking and shite at neets wen thoo's dun"! - the fallacy of the easy going farmers and labourers was soon dispelled when you really got amongst the animals, the fields of turnips and hay. One benevolent farmer was heard say that Sunday was 'lig in' day and as long as the lads were out of their beds by 5 a.m. for milking, feeding etc. he was quite happy. The narrow margin of going to and getting out of bed sometimes did an overlap when there was difficulty in ascertaining whether you were coming or going. For instance, a friend of mine nearly jumped out of his skin one morning, when the loud bang-bang of his bedroom door and the farmer's "Come 'ee lad is ta' in bed?" brought forth his reply, "No, nut yit"! He had been to one of the village 'hops' and maybe dawdled awhile on the way home with some farm lass.

These 'hops' were quite something when Ladies Choice became 'T' Lassies Pick' or the more crude version 'T' Heifer's Grab'. It was advisable for the girls to wear shin-guards when the heavy hob-nailed boots attempted the light fantastic. There was always a general melee when the dance finished around midnight, when the lads would. try 'carting off' the lady of their choice. One night a few of we younger lads followed a well known Don Juan, who fancied himself no end (this lad had a face like a pound of bacon and patent leather hair which was well-greased with a good brand of axle grease). We crept up on them to hear him whispering words of love in her lug like "Dost ta still love us, lass?"; "Aye" was the reply. "Then hod thee girt gob up and a'hl gie thee a kiss"' Proper romantic stuff. Our loud guffaws soon gave the game away and broke the spell for the two romantics so much so, that instead of getting something, he got nowt! We were chased from the scene by the red-faced Lothario and never did find out what the 'something' was.

A great day out was the local Agricultural Show when the gentry got their feet in the sludge with the ordinary farm 'yocks'. I remember once being given the choice of any animal on the farm to show in its appropriate class. The farmer would pay the entry for me. I chose a black hornless Aberdeen Angus Heifer and spent some hours washing down and grooming until it shone like silk. I showed quite a few bruises at the end of this grooming operation and that was before we even set off on the two miles trudge through the country lanes to the Show-Ground. The animal resented the indignity of the head collar and did its best to climb over the hedge every twenty yards or so. By the time I reached the Show Ground I was a lather of sweat and completely exhausted, but nevertheless, gave the black so and so another polish up with the piece of 'Uveco' bag I carried for the purpose. Lo and behold, in the class of 20 or so beasts my charge had the blue rosette of 2nd fastened to the head-collar. The farmer had been watching intently whilst the judging was taking place and every now and again directing me to "Gie it a la'll pat on 't arse"! When the order of judging was being lined up for the prize presentations and it was obvious that my black beauty was very well placed the farmer decided to duck under the ropes into the ring and take over the animal from me. The rosette was affixed to the head collar but the farmer held out his hand for the 5/- prize money. I was given 6d for one of my hardest days on the farm. Big deal! After the Show I took the beast a little way up the road and bunged it into a field before proceeding back to the village to enjoy the fruits of my labour - all 6d of it! It must have been the homing version of the bovine breed because it eventually made it's way back to the farm a couple of days later, much to the delight of the farmer who had been informed that the 'Aberdeen' had broken away from me and was last seen heading in the opposite direction. I considered I had been cheated, but hired hands had no right to complain. Giving the cat a hefty kick could possibly relieve the tension.

In spite of the more obvious draw-backs of the system, on the whole, I was quite happy on this farm and became very fond of the two year old twin daughters, who would attach themselves to me at every opportunity. I had to constantly dodge them to carry out my normal duties. The farm buildings were absolutely ridden with rats which would be scrambling all round the byre troughs, whilst milking was in progress. They had absolutely no fear of humans and would walk over your feet. At first there was a revulsion and fear of these pests but after a while you just came to accept their presence.

In those days it was the practice for farmers to give a home to dogs from the local Hunt pack, during the non-hunting time of the year or the 'off' season. Where possible, terriers and hounds were allocated the same lodge. We had a rugged, battle scarred terrier known as Tyke and he had a constant running fight with the rat pack. One day I was sitting milking and feeling a little drowsy owing to the warmth generated by the cows in the small byre, when in came Tyke to have a go at the rats. Well, although the cows would accept the presence of the rats there was no similar acceptance of dogs and when Tyke made his attach on a couple of rats just to my rear, the cow gave me a real 'fourpenny one' with its rear leg and bounced me across the byre right in line for another one from the cow opposite. I felt like the ball in a tennis match before sprawling in the sloppy cow dung with the milk bucket round my neck like a soft collar. What with the half bucket of milk all over me and the cow dung splattered here and there I was in a right state, so much so, that I had to wash down fully clothed at the water trough in the yard. Tyke had the cheek to approach me with wagging tail and the pleased look of the conqueror. Although I loved the dog I didn't love it *that* much and surprised him by booting him up the posterior.

The foxhound we boarded was one 'Miller' and a beautiful white young dog he was too. He would go off across the 'Flats' on a one dog hunt. It was amusing to watch the antics of this animal when he would 'put up' a rabbit or hare, sit on his rump howling before pursuing his quarry. By the time these preliminaries were completed, the rabbit or hare would be miles away. We once got him all spruced up for the Rydal Show, shampooed with good old carbolic soap, toe-nails, teeth - the lot. This was the evening before the Show and after the big clean up Miller was bedded down in the straw in a stone building adjoining the barn. 'Miller' had other ideas and during the night he ate his way through the shuttered window and set off over the 'Flats' in a raging thunder storm. I could hear him baying during the night but could do nothing about it until next morning. He returned in a dreadful state and there was just time to slosh him down with buckets of water before the pick up wagon arrived. The handler must have done a good job on him during the 20 miles journey because he was the best in his class and, in fact, was the 'Best In Show', hunting dog classes. He was a beautiful dog with a nature to match.

On The 'Parish'

By the time I was 17 years old I was heartily sick of being on 24 hour 'beck and call' for a mere pittance, so I decided to retire from work on the land. It didn't take a mathematical genius to work out that the 8/- a week on the 'Parish' was better than the five or six shillings a week earned on slave labour.. For the 8/- we had to attend the Market Hall for various activities comprising of P.T., shoe and clog mending, joiner work, hair cutting etc. This was for a five day week starting 9 a.m. and finishing 4 p.m. Bread and jam sandwiches were taken by most, but if anyone had ham or cheese it was automatically assumed that they had robbed a bank. Given the right feeding we would have been the fittest and strongest lads in the land. There were various loaning out jobs, where, of the 200 or so attendants there would be a turnip snagging, haytiming etc. (back to the land again) where maybe 10 men would be required. There was a general rush to get to the back of the queue, feign a limp or wrap an old rag round the hand. The farmers were on a good thing here because you even had to take your own buttees and hope that a hot drink would be supplied. I can't help thinking that someone, somewhere, was getting a back hander and I don't mean a smack in the puss.

One of my friends had been on a job for a week or so and when I asked the nature of the job, he told me he had been washing the inmates of the local Workhouse! Apparently these were 'gentlemen of the road', who refused to bath until intimidated by six or so 'washers'. Ned said they would fill the big communal bath - laced with plenty of disinfectant and then proceed to shove the 'inmates' through as if they were sheep going through the sheep dipping pens. Dignity of the human species was not considered in those days.

Boxing was the favourite sport and one can only think that participation was an outlet for an inbuilt aggression due to a lot of unjustified poverty. Chips just don't grow on shoulders overnight. The pity of it was we had to take it out of each other whilst the various Government factions belted each other with balloons on sticks before going off together for lunch. A yard of silver tongue oratory didn't amount to an inch of action and did nothing towards wiping out the Dole queue, the Means Test or the indignity of applying for Parish Relief. So much for some of the reasons for stimulating an interest in the 'noble art'. Many's the times I have climbed up into the loft behind P.A. Burn's pub on Jacktrees Road to mix with some of the local 'white hopes'. I must have been mad because some of these lads could really go and it was no disgrace to be on the wrong end of a left hook or a straight left but even this knowledge didn't relieve the pain. This boxing school was run by Willie Adair who had managed to beg, borrow or steal an assortment of gym equipment which was very primitive, to say the least. One 56lb. weight for swinging round with the teeth (to strengthen the neck and jaw muscles), one sand bag (filled) for slamming into the 'wall of 6' stomach muscles and two sets of boxing gloves. Methinks a bag of fish and chips would have been a better build up for muscle. One memorable occasion was when we hired the Market Hall to put on a boxing exhibition which was hilarious from the first bell. I was to fight a chap with quite a reputation and the terrifying name of Slasher! The name itself overawed me and when he came in at me grunting all sorts of animal noises all I wanted to do was dive through the ropes for safety. Before I could persuade my legs to move he had planted two in the solar plexus and one on my right ear. The last blow should have been on the chin but the two in the stomach had decided for me that the canvas was the only safe place in the Hall. Even then I thought there was a chance he could kick me because he was really going berserk, waving his arms above the head to the howling spectators and doing all sorts of doubling shuffling manoeuvres with his feet. I don't think he liked me and I had never seen the chap in my life! I think if I had stopped down there was a good chance of him breaking a leg or something with his fancy footwork. However, pride dictated to me that I must get up and make a fight of it, and this I did for three painful rounds. The three rounds seemed like three months to me and I was so far behind on points my seconds told me that if I knocked my opponent out I would probably get a draw. I offered to change places with one of the seconds but he didn't seem interested. I got a rousing ovation to go with my split lips, bruised face and loose teeth. My opponent by now had been coaxed back to nearly human behaviour and he proceeded to give me a big hug of commiseration. I resisted the impulse to kick him in the crutch - but only just! The follow on bout was even more hilarious when the local comedian Rusty Meagan met another pugilistic monster. I don't know where they found them all! Rusty set off at a run on the first tinkle of the timekeeper's bell and never stopped running except to step through the ropes now and again to avoid the flailing arms of his opponent. The only time Rusty showed any aggression was between the rounds when he kept taunting his opponent, but as soon as the bell went it was on the bike again! I think Rusty got one smack in and that was when his opponent was on his way back to his corner at the end of the round. He belted him one behind the ear and I think the intention was to get disqualified. The referee pretended he wasn't looking and Rusty had to carry on running for the termination of the bout.

As well as boxing we did P.T. displays and gymnastic techniques. One hair-raising stunt was to jump over ten or twelve lined up sitting forms much the same as the barrel jumping skaters or in fact Evil Knievel doing the bus jump. The only difference here was that we made contact with the far edge of the end form and did a back lift on to the feet. The contact had to be a split second judgement or there was a good chance of breaking the neck.

Sooner or later there had to be an end to this meaningless existence and the realisation that there was the likelihood of aimlessly going through life and getting nowhere fast. Just at this time I had an Uncle finishing his time in the East Lancs. Regt. who arrived home from India with tales of action on the N.W. Frontier, the Khyber Pass, Deolali and many other exotic names. To someone who had never been further than a Sunday School trip to Seascale, the tales made a great impression and so the seed was sown to grab the chance to travel into the great unknown. Two pals and myself decided to go down to the Whitehaven

Drill Hall and offer our services to the King. When the day came one of the lads got cold feet, but the other agreed to go through with it. Now this chap had the worst impediment in speech I have ever heard and but for knowing him all his life there would be very little communication. The outcome was that he failed his medical but complained bitterly and suggested that you didn't have to talk the enemy to death but simply to shoot them. However, of the three original musketeers I became a loner and as I have said earlier, had hardly been outside my own village except for the Sunday School trips which were sometimes a ten mile train ride down the coast to Seascale, or on some occasions it was a 'trip to Dent'. I kept saying to myself, "What have I done? What have I done?". However the King's shilling had been accepted and all I had to do was to go home and await the call. It was a few days before I could bring myself to tell my Father, but when I did, he agreed that I had made a sensible decision. The day afterwards I received a buff envelope enclosing a travel warrant to proceed from Whitehaven to Ashton-Under-Lyne. I had nothing to pack except a tooth brush and shaving gear which I shoved in my pocket. I stepped down from our front doorstep one very cold and snowy morning around 6.30 a.m., the date: 6th December 1933. There was a walk of 6 miles facing me in the black dark, but fortune smiled on me (for once) when a flat platform wagon pulled up alongside and offered a lift to the station. It was a West Cumb. Farmers' wagon and driven by one of the village men lucky enough to have a job, 'Sep' Bawden.

I was now really and truly flying from the nest, and my own man from that time on.

Ladysmith Barracks

After a thousand enquiries en route as to where I changed trains, which platform etc. a very hungry 18 year old arrived in this town in the late afternoon. I hadn't a halfpenny in my pocket to buy food on the journey but hunger was no stranger to me. I reported to the Guard Room and was directed first to the Dining Hall for a mug of hot sweet tea and two slices of bread and dripping. It was nectar to me. There were a few more mufti clothed recruits and we did a bit of bashful introductions, before being shown the Barrack rooms and beds comprising of three 'biscuits' and a hard pillow. The first night was a very restless time and not helped by the fact that faint sobbing could be heard from different beds. The home-sick bug had struck and I'm not ashamed to say I was that way myself. It was just starting to sink in that I had signed on for 7 years with the 'Colours' and 5 years on the reserve. It seemed a lifetime, and, as it turned out very nearly was.

After a restless night it was 'hands off your levers and feet on the floor' when the bugle reminded us that we were in the Army boy! The bugler had hardly taken a deep breath to blow reveille when the door was slammed open and this red-sashed character stood screaming and shouting in a foreign language. After a while it dawned on us that he required that the windows be opened wide to the elements and that the floor resembled a lumber camp, also that the barrack room smelt like a whore's garret. The explanation for the lumber camp remark was that one of the lads had thrown a matchstick on the floor, but how he managed to marry the whore's garret with a lumber camp was beyond me. I thought I had been admitted to the 'giggle factory' and expected some white smocked orderly to dash in with a hypodermic syringe, but after giving myself a smack on the side of the head it all came back to me and I knew I was well and truly hooked.

Rivalry between the various 30 man squads was fostered by the Squad Sgts. both on and off parade. We had overnight raids when Somme Squad would gum shoe into the domain of Marne Squad or Guadaloupe Squad in the early hours, each man being allocated a certain bed to up end. If you were unlucky enough to draw for the furthest from the only door outlet you had to be prepared to punch your way out. Capture meant a dragging to the ablution basins and either doused with buckets of icy water or forcibly held under the cold showers. Things got to such a pass that each squad had a sentry system of one man being detailed to pull his bed across the door entry and sleep with one eye open and both ears, but what with the coming and going of the weak bladdered, things could get a bit confusing. It was not unknown for a poor innocent squaddie to be on the receiving end of a bayonet like thrust with a floor mop. Injuries incurred on these skirmishes would never be described as such but rather the result of falling down the stone stairs or tripping over a bucket. Our respective Squad Sgts. would instill into us that we were the best squad in the best Company in the best Battalion, and the best Regiment in the best Army in the world - The British Army! Olé!

Sarcasm was very sharp and mickey taking was common practice. One of our lads swears the following dialogue took place.

Sgt.: "Wakey, Wakey sleepy head, time to rise"

Recruit: "But I don't wish to rise!"

Sgt.: "What! When all the little birds are singing!"

Recruit: "**** the little Dicky birds!"

Sgt.: "Sarge is going to be very angry and hand you over to the Bogy man who will cut off all your hair and put you in his Hotel".

Recruit: "No, don't Sarge. I swear on Cubs honour to be good".

Sgt.: "All right, then. Up's a daisy. Let's see how we can make our buttons and shoes all nice and shiny like a shitty stick".

After being 'fell in' on the holiest of holy parade ground and sorted out in order of size and religion this motley cross section of the community were collectively introduced to our, Father, mother, confessor and judge going by the terrifying name of 'Tiger' Kirk. We were informed by this terrifying apparition that we were all crows, but before he had finished with us we would be clockwork soldiers, who would jump under a bus if ordered to do so without question. This bloke must have been reading Rudyard Kipling, 'Ours not to reason why, ours but to do and die'. Looking at him I wouldn't have thought a gentle pastime like reading would be part of his curriculum. We were then marched or ,to be more exact, ushered in the general direction of the Depot barber's shop. This man was a sadist although he thought he was the world's greatest comedian. The first man in the chair had a beautiful head of blond curly hair to which this Sweeny Todd took instant exception, first by starting at the front of the hair line and pushing the clippers right over the top of the head and down to the nape of the neck, cutting some, pulling some. He then proceeded from behind one ear and once again over the head and down behind the other ear.

Then he stood back to admire his handiwork and informing the rest of us that it was the 'hot cross bun' crop but if we wished we could have the stipulated short back and sides with the main crop on the top of the head not to exceed one inch. Under the watchful gaze of 'Tiger' we all readily agreed.

The twenty or so recruits hadn't time to warm the chair before being bundled out for the next victim. Every one had to hold down their own ears to save time. The barber was more a work-study estimator than a barber. The first hair cut was 'on the house' but all subsequent clips were 2d each, and the Tiger made sure that we were checked for a hair-cut about once per week. He was on a commission basis and with beer at 4d a pint it meant that we were responsible for his many hang-overs and fiendish temper displays. The thoughts of being under Tiger's tender care for 26 weeks was terrible and one or two of the lads decided to take off ostensibly to join the French Foreign Legion, where they would have had an easier time. However, those that soldiered on gradually realised that there was a heart under the big chest of Tiger's tunic. If any of 'his lads' got in any sort of trouble and provided they were not contravening Military law he would fight tooth and claw for them. I had personal proof of this when I was whipped into the Guardhouse for 'dumb insolence'. I didn't think this charge was possible but there I was behind the bars to prove it was. I was only in half an hour when Tiger missed my homely face in his squad. I was out and back on the hallowed ground of the Barrack Square in about two minutes flat and I wasn't sure whether to be pleased or not. The Corporal who had placed me in the 'Clink' was sporting a black eye the following day!

One of our squad members was a native of Gretna and was the most awkward of recruits. It looked like his arms and legs had just been stuck on with drawing pins. On the command of 'Quick March' he would set off with the same arm swinging in unison to the same leg and attempting to correct by changing step which would practically tie him in knots. The more Tiger screamed the more flustered became Jock and his face assumed the same scarlet hue as his hair. Came the time when Jock had to parade on his own after we had done our normal stint of square bashing. The Corporal detailed for this extra duty was none too pleased about it and he hit on a novel idea for correcting Jock's lack of co-ordination. He went down to the stables and returned with sane hay in one hand and straw in the other, which he then proceeded to stuff under the bottom of Jock's puttees. Hay under one puttee and straw under the other, after first ascertaining that Jock knew the difference. He then did the same with the tunic sleeves so that it was straw in right leg, straw in left arm, hay in left leg and hay in right hand. The exercise then commenced with the word of command. "Hay foot! Straw foot! Hay foot! Straw foot!". After a while jock got the hang of it and never looked back! The Corporal was always called 'Hay-foot' from that day on.

We were under the constant eye of Tiger who was determined that Somme Squad would be the smartest bunch of men in the whole British

Army on or off parade.

I started getting quite keen on the soldiering lark and fancied myself as an unpaid, unwanted, uncouth L/Corporal, in fact, I was on the short list of candidates until I blotted my copy book by trying too hard. The incident happened one pay parade when we were being paid out in the big indoor Drill shed because of inclement weather. The floor of this huge building comprised wooden block sets which had been highly polished with many years of use. Tiger was standing behind the young Subaltern who sat on a chair on the right flank of the Pay Sgt. with the money was on a table in front of them. My name was called out and under the watchful gaze of Tiger I became flustered and somehow or other managed to get one foot behind the heel of the other foot which sent me in a head long dive towards the pay table!! They must have thought it was a smash and grab because I was instantly surrounded by screaming N.C.O.'s. I lost all interest in promotion from that time on. What else?

Came the day when all the Squad were double marched down to the Gym and made climb on to scales ostensibly to check our weight. In effect that was the idea but the reason was more sinister when 'Tiger' marked on his big 'name list' words like 'Lightweight, Welterweight, Middle and Light Heavy weight'. "But, I don't box, Sergeant". "Correction, you maybe didn't up to now, but as from now you are an up and coming Battalion, Light weight Champion and just starting on a long run of victories"! Now my earlier experience of Market Hall thumping had me in with some experience at least, but some of these other lads had never seen boxing gloves let alone worn them. Nevertheless all were entered in the pre-lims and the big thump out began with flailing arms, back-handers, low punches - the lot. The Marquis of Queensbury had never heard of some of these punches. One thing for sure, if you were getting a hammering you had to go down fighting, unless the corner 'second' threw in the towel and then you had to be at death's door. After three fights or brawls I was chosen to represent my squad in the Novices section but came unstuck in the final when I met this iron man, who had muscles in his spit. How in Heaven's name he had managed to manipulate the scales on the weigh in was a mystery, because he looked all of 11 stones against my $9^1/2$ stones. Anyhow, I dodged, ducked and weaved my way through the three rounds, and was delighted that I had only a few superficial injuries like a broken nose, split eye-brows and injured pride. I was adjudged to be a little behind on points, but feel sure that with a bit more luck (like Boyo dropping dead or something) I would have got the verdict.

The 26 weeks Depot training at last came to an end and the end result was 30 robots who could do arms drill or foot drill with Guards' like precision and a fierce pride in the uniform and the Battalion. On the day of 'passing out' the Tiger joined us in our canteen and accepted pints from all and sundry. Accepted, mind you, not pay for any. He drank like he had hollow legs and all the time his big face getting more crimson by the minute. Before the night was over we had the Tiger standing on a chair and demonstrating the various techniques of the 'one man band' at the singing "Cheer up, me lads.... 'em all". We finished up with 'Nellie Dean' and then a rousing chorus of 'For he's a jolly good fellow'. We *must* have been drunk. I'm sure there were tears in his eyes when he bid us farewell in his own inimitable style: "Get fell in you horrible crows; what are you!!?", "Crows, sergeant!" was the quick reply. I don't think the tears were so much for seeing us off but maybe the thought of having to tackle another 30 or so awkward civilians and having to explain to them that although they had all broken their mother's hearts they wouldn't break his. Looking at the motley crew just 'falling in' I wouldn't have taken any bets on the outcome!

Strensall Camp

A higgledy piggledy collection of new brick type Barrack rooms and 1914/1918 war wooden huts raised on brick plinths, looking for all the world as if they had all been taken up on a giant sky lift and dropped at random. This was to be our home for the next four years. To the 'townies' the bleak open country side presented a formidable picture, and after the comparative closed-in intimacy of Ladysmith Barracks, it was as if we had been dumped in an oasis in the outback. The friendships which had been cemented during our Depot training were now to be broken up by the dispersal of our group to the four main Companies - A, B, C and D. Even in the allotted Companies there was a further break up to Platoons and Sections. New 'mukkers' had to be made and there was always the enterprising boyo who would show you round with the priority given to the N.A.A.F.I., where there was a goodly assortment of 'cha and wads' (tea and cakes). If it was possible to push through the

N.A.A.F.I. sheiks at the counter and catch the eye of one of the lovesick N.A.A.F.I. girls, one could get a mug of tea and anything from bread and jam fritters to rock cakes (a very apt name too). 1d for tea and 1d for cake. The basic wage was 2/- per day and qualification increments for 'sharp-shooting', physical adaption and a general all round awareness as befits the good soldier. It was possible to reach the high rate of 3/- per day but out of this wage some of us had made 'allotments' of 6d per day to fathers, mothers or whatever. Then there was the expense of metal polish, white Blanco, green Blanco, shoe and chin-strap polish etc. There was a monthly Credit/Debit check, when each man had to sign for the written figure after a further reduction for the mythical Barrack Room Damages. If a window was broken and honourably reported by the 'victim' he had to pay twice over; once for the original window and once for a new replacement. The mind boggles! This unfair situation cut down the 'honourables' by about $99^{1}/2\%$ and no wonder.

Discipline was very strict indeed, the age old excuse being put forward that in 'the field' under active conditions there was a greater welding together, and orders of manoeuvre being carried out without question made for success. Nevertheless, some of the so-called military crimes were very petty. A dirty cap badge could carry three days 'jankers'* or failure to salute an officer could mean seven days 'jankers'. This meant that for the termination of the C.B. (confined to Barracks) the poor soldier had to answer the bugle call every half hour during the 'off duty' hours when others were playing sport, going to the N.A.A.F.I. or even going down town on pass. The 'Jankers' bugle call was a distinctive call and had to be answered 'on the double', each half hour being in different equipment or dress. The culprits had to form up in front of the Guard House and be inspected by the Guard Cmmdr., who decided on the next mode of presentation. It was a full half hour's job getting ready for the next call and the run in was punishment in itself especially in 'full bumper', i.e. full equipment of webbing complete with rifle. The last call of the punishment was always celebrated with a few pints at the N.A.A.F.I. or as some old soldiers said 'bashing the coir' or resting on the bed. The whole of our lives was devoted to one aim - getting fit and keeping fit. Every one had to have a go at one sporting activity or another with the exception of the over thirty's, who

---

* Jankers - confined to barracks.

were considered to be too old! I had always been something of a sportsman and represented the Battalion at Football, Hockey, Athletics by way of 440, 880 yards, and Cross Country running. I also held the Long Jump record for years (22 feet). This distance is now being jumped by the 'weaker' sex. In spite of my earlier days being somewhat disastrous I still enjoyed competing in the Boxing competitions and eventually won my weight in the Opens (welter-weight).

In 1936 Mussolini was kicking the sand around in the Middle East and it was decided to send reinforcements out to Egypt. By this time I had been transferred to the Battalion Signal Section and the 'iddy umpty' was giving me the hump. So much so that I volunteered for drafting abroad. My application was turned down along with a few more battalion footballers, who at that time were doing well in the Army Cup matches. I ask you? Anyhow, we just reached the semi-final before being knocked out in extra time. When the Draft for the Middle East was published my 'mukker' and I were not on the list. We were desperately disappointed and decided to drown our sorrows in the drinking dens of York City. We not only drowned our sorrows but managed to get slung in the local 'cooler' after having a running fight with members of the Fighting Fifth (Northumberland Fusiliers). We came round the following morning all battered and bruised, lying in a cell and puzzling on the notice attached to the cell wall which stated 'Finger Prints Need Not Be Given By First Offenders'. The police were surprisingly very kind and brought us steaming mugs of sweet tea with plenty of toasted bread. I though this was maybe the last meal before hanging because up to then everything was hazy and no reason had been given for our detention. We were eventually led up the little stairway into the box facing a bench of J.P.'s or Magistrates, one of them being Miss Rowntree (Chocolate). The charge was read out to the effect that we instigated a brawl in their fair city (the very words) and had afterwards resisted arrest. We apologised for our out of character behaviour (we had to, because one of our Officers was sat in the Well of the Court) and after a run down of the history of the City and all the angels who dwelt therein, we were handed over to the Military authorities. There was no secret made of the fact that troops were all right if confined to their own Barracks precinct, but not much liked roaming the City. Of course that was before the war when Tommy was neither 'this' nor 'that'.

I was on Christmas leave in 1937 and really living it up in my two village pubs with a bit of 'square pushing' on the side. I rather fancied myself in uniform Khaki, white belt and swagger cane. Well, if you don't think you are just great at 23, then you never will, so I make no excuse for the vanity.

Only just squeezing my head down the stairs one morning I was confronted with an ominous looking buff envelope, the contents of which instructed that I return to my Unit forthwith. I was to proceed on a motor cycle dispatch rider's course to Catterick Camp and any outstanding leave would be granted on the termination of the three month's course. Although I wasn't keen on tearing myself away from the flesh-pots of the village I rather looked forward to being a glamourous Despatch Rider. To say we were taught to ride a motor cycle would be a gross understatement. We were attached to the 4th Tank Corps exhibition team. These lads gave riding thrills all over the world and had to ride backwards, frontwards, upside down, jumping through flames and a variety of riding techniques. We all rode Norton 500cc bikes and they were extremely nippy for the times. All preliminary training was carried out on the tank training area of Waitewith Bank which overlooked this vast Barracks complex. The first week or so was a succession of thrills and spills and most of the pupils walking round like retired cowboys looking for a horse. We gradually got the hang of it and within a month were riding like Cossacks. Once again I made an unlucky move and I *do* believe I had a bad-luck angel sitting on my shoulders. It happened this way. The mud spattered bikes were all up on the stands with engines ticking over and engaged in low gear. Sticking strictly to the Army tradition of everything being 'in line' we proceeded to hose the bikes down whilst the off the ground rear wheels were in motion. I was at the very end and the first to use the hose before handing over to the next in line. What happened next was chaotic when I pushed my bike forward without thinking to knock it out of gear. The handlebars shot out of my hands and the resulting knock-on saw ten bikes shooting off on their own with frantic drivers trying to catch them. To make matters worse the area around the wash down taps was a sheet of ice. Everyone was jumping about like the Keystone Cops and I'm sure Candid Camera would have had a field day. The Battery Sgt. Major was a witness to this incident and it was then I realised that even Sgt. Majors can be human. He stood holding his sides and laughing his head off! Little damage was done and it was just accepted as being one of those things which happen to any one. Compared to our own Unit the discipline here was much more relaxed and we were sorry when the course came to an end. All passed the riding test with honours and our conduct whilst being attached to the Tank Corps. was said to be exemplary. This pleased our own Unit C.O. very much but we never did get our outstanding leave. Just to prove that I was prone to accidents, there were two incidents which happened to me within a very short time of my return to the Unit. We had sallied forth to celebrate our return to the fold and decided on a night out to the Yearsley Grove Hotel on the roadside near Huntington. We had a good old booze up and a bit of skylarking before being shown the door at 10.00 p.m. It was a real black dark night and away from the pub premises it was difficult to see much. I had a brand new 50/- suit on and really felt great. There were about ten of us and we decided to walk a mile or so down the road to a local dance hall En route there were many calls of nature owing to the vast quantities of beer consumed by all and sundry. I had just got my bearings and stepped off the road behind an electrical distribution box. Next thing I know I am flat on my back in an extremely muddy, rain water ditch! I was like a rugby league player when I clambered out, and it didn't help matters when the rest of the company fell about laughing. There I was dripping mud from my brand new 50/- Tailor's suit - five miles from Barracks and on my way to a knees up! Fortunately, one of the lads had a girlfriend living near by and I was invited into the house by her kind hearted Mother who provided me with a blanket while she made some attempt to clean up the 'whistle and flute'. It was some hours before I could get things sorted out and by that time I was well and truly A.W.O.L.* and a five miles walk back to Strensall facing me. The rest of the lads had carried on to the dance and caught the last bus around midnight but I was on my Tod. Nevertheless I decided to face the music and reported to the Guard Cmmdr. around 2.00 a.m. He was one of the battalion football team and a good guy, so he decided that I sneak back to my billet whilst he cooked the 'pass in books'. That little kindness saved me seven days jankers - I never forgot him for it. The suit, incidentally, was sent to the cleaners but in the process managed to shrink about two sizes. I sold it for 10/- to a bloke who was not entitled to wear

* A.W.O.L. - Absent without leave.

44

civilian clothes at the time but who had decided to desert. The suit must have brought good luck to him because his desertion was successful.

The other incident happened one Sunday afternoon shortly afterwards when three of us decided to do a little boating on the Ouse. None of us had ever rowed before, but a little thing like that didn't deter us. We pushed off from the bank and 'caught crabs' all the way upstream for a few hundred yards before becoming exhausted and heading for a tie up on the river bank. It was a lovely sunny day as we lay back, smoking a woodbine and wishing the day would never end. Eventually we had to clamber aboard and head downstream or be charged extra hiring time for the craft. I was the second man to climb aboard and promptly untied the rope preparatory to the third member coming. Just as he was putting his foot on board he realised that he had left his cap on the river bank. By this time I was holding two handsful of grass and trying to hold the boat, but the current was very strong and my holding on became a lying on with the boat moving further and further from the side. You've guessed it? Right first time! Straight down in about 8ft of water dressed in full uniform, puttees, white belt - the lot. My cap was the only thing on the surface when I eventually battled my way to the river side. The bloke in the boat was shouting his head off and trying to control the clumsy craft with one oar, the other having gone over the side with me. When I got the water out of my ears and got my bearings I squelched my way down stream and attempted to attract the attention of the boat owners to indicate that my mate was on his way to the Pacific unless apprehended. The boat owner then set off in pursuit in his little outboard motored craft and managed to grab the runaway vessel. He also retrieved my cap along with the drifting oar. He doubled the hire charge to recompense for his near heart attack and for retrieving my cap, but we were glad to pay. I had to ride home on the bus and when I got off my seat at the Barracks entrance the conductor glared at me because I had left a big wet patch on his seat. I told him I had malaria because by this time I was shivering like a dog passing bones. I don't know whether he believed me or not and what's more I was past caring.

Aldershot (Tournai)

I can't say I was sorry to see the last of Strensall Camp when we formed up in order of convoy one cold and bitter day in March 1938.

By then I was a Despatch Rider, first class, and quite enjoyed blasting back and forward from North Command (York) to Strensall Camp. Every bend and bump in the road was a challenge to my riding ability and time was the enemy. Anyhow, the first day's ride was from Strensall to Lichfield, each vehicle to be 180 yds apart, D.R.'s to ensure a straight and trouble free run. There were one or two minor bumps on the way and plenty of abuse from other users of the road, but they were in the minor league compared to the Army. The ability to read a map was a priority because all troop movements by road had to be off the main thoroughfare and it was the D.R.'s job to shoot ahead in turn and control traffic through the country lanes. No M6, M5 or whatever in those days. The first night was spent at Lichfield and I was never so cold after riding most of the way. One of our lads had to be lifted off the saddle and it took a hot shower before all feelings returned to the limbs.

An early start next morning saw us on the road to our journey's end - Aldershot. This must have been the most hated place in the whole of the Army billeting set up. It was just one vast Barracks, and there was never the feeling of relaxing even when on civilian pass. In fact, it seemed a waste of time getting into civilian clothes just to go to the Wellington Cinema, known to the troops as the 'Gaff'. The right arm was never still saluting the dozens of Officers all over the place. One thing for sure, it was possible to buy the best pies ever tasted from a chap with an ice cream like van. His name to us was 'Pie Tommy' and he would hold the pie in his left hand with thumb of the right hand poised in a downward direction over the pie. "With or without?" he would question. If the request was "With", he would penetrate the top of the pie with the thumb and fill the hole up with hot brown gravy. Delicious, they were. The thumb was always clean because he would lick it before attacking the next pie. I never knew this lack of hygiene harm anyone in the slightest. So he must have licked it good and clean!

The unexpected happened to me within a few weeks of our arrival in Tournai Barracks. I got promotion to unpaid L/Cpl! I wrote and told my Father of this promotion but advised him not to alter his life style as yet, and he could still continue talking to the neighbours. The second stripe was the one that counted and from that time there would have to be no fraternising with the common peasants. I didn't have the unpaid stripe

---

* Ram Sammi - Hindustani slang for 'Booze up'.

for long owing to a misunderstanding with the Batt. Drum Major. It was a Sunday morning and the morning after a 'Ram Sammi'* in the N.A.A.F.I. the night previous. There was the greatest reluctance to "Wakey, wakey, rise and shine, come away there! Stowaway those f........ flea bags!" The Drum Major was the acting Orderly Sgt. for that day and his first duty was to see that the Company had their feet on the floor on the instant he started slamming the Barrack Room door. The Bugler had hardly started with the hated 'Charlie, Charlie, get out of bed', when the door was nearly knocked off the hinges and this bellowing figure demanded we be instantly awake, dressed and outside in five minutes! You had to work a shave into the five minutes in ice cold tap water. When he left the Barrack Room I jokingly shouted to the rest of the occupants "Up!, Up!, Up!... I'll give you 25 minutes to get out of these beds!!" This before submerging under the bed clothes again. Unfortunately, 'Drummy' heard me and he doubled back note-book at the ready and the request that everyone stayed exactly where they were until he got all the names and numbers. The outcome of this tomfoolery was to be named as the leader of a mutiny. What a stupid charge for such a trivial matter. The R.S.M. nearly had a duck fit when he saw the charge and the 15 culprits were wheeled up to his office for an enquiry. The charge was subsequently changed to hesitating to obey an order given by a superior officer. I saw the slightest flicker of amusement cross his face when hearing of my remark but he wasn't so amused as to let the charge drop. First of all, I was stripped of rank. Blimey, the stitching had hardly settled down before it was off again. The whole 15 of us then got 3 days jankers and if you haven't seen 15 frantic squaddies, all trying to get down the same flight of stairs at the same time, you ain't seen anything!

It was a constant run from the end of normal parade times until lights out with no time even for supper. After missing this meal the first day I asked for an interview with the R.S.M. and put forward on behalf of us all that missing a meal was not part of our punishment. I thought the roof had fallen in and I couldn't make out a word he had said. He must have been heard in the next block of Barrack rooms, because the blokes were all crowding the windows just in time to see me doubling back to my billet *and* at the full knees bend! I thought I was taking up my 'mad horse' career again. The interview bore some fruit, however, when there was a cut back of one janker call to allow us to have our supper meal.

Shortly after this episode I was to go on a Hygiene course to the 'School of Hygiene'. Pupils were drawn from every Unit in the Army and we had a great time travelling the country side in a couple of 15 cwt trucks and a water tanker in tow. We would stop anywhere there was a good supply of water, ditches, canals or ponds. We would then filter draw the Tanker full of dirty looking water and carry out what was known as the Horrocks Test to determine the amount of purifying powder required to make it fit for human consumption. Some of the water was putrid when we sucked it into the tank, and not much better when we had supplied the magic formula. However, we had to boil up and make our own brew with the filthy stuff and nobody got typhoid, phystosomiases, 'lurgy lurgy' or 'dum, dum', the credit for which being to our skill but I rather think the boil up did the trick.

I struck up a friendship with a Jock of the Gordon Highlanders and just to relieve the monotony, Jock and I decided to swap uniforms. Many of the other pupils followed suit and there was all sorts of skylarking going on. I had a mop under the arm, and making all sorts of bagpipe noises when the roll call whistle was blown by the Educational Sergeant. We had no time to get sorted out so just fell in outside the billet. When the Sergeant started calling the roll he thought he had the wrong list when one of the Manchesters answered the name in Highland kilt, the same for the other pupils who were Leicesters dressed like Surreys. I hate to think what situation would have developed if there had been a W.A.A.F. detachment. To start with the Sergeant was exasperated but saw the funny side of it later. He got his own back on me the following day which was a 'Bull' day for some visiting celebrity. He detailed me to take the key for the Entomological Lab. to dust and clean up but not to go into the room at the rear of the Lab. Of course I went in and got the biggest fright of my life. The room was fairly dark and I had to grope around for the light switch. On turning round to scan the room I was faced with this monstrous man-sized insect with big bulbous eyes! I nearly passed out with shock before hitting the door at a high rate of knots. The Sergeant knew I would have to be nosey and enter the room and was waiting for me coming out. After calming me down he took a grip on my shaking arms and led me back inside to introduce me to 'Mozzy' this being a full scale model of a Mosquito, used in medical and scientific studies. I could have blocked him there and then until he called me Jock and then the penny dropped. Whether

48

he was making recompense for this action or whether it was genuine he was to give me top marks at the end of the course.

Sailing On To Singapore

In September of 1938 a Draft list came out and I was included, this after volunteers were called for. We marched out of Tournai Barracks one bright morning headed by the Band and Drums and entrained for Southampton. The thumping drums did nothing to alleviate the hangover which followed the canteen booze up of the night previous. Just to show how everyone's life is ruled by fate, the following incidences were brought back to me many years later.

The Corporal on Canteen duties that evening was a townie of mine (Jock Hardy), and he certainly worked for his living that night owing to a couple of up ended tables and a situation which developed into a 'free for all'. Jock did his best to sort things out but was catching it from both sides. The Regimental Police had to be eventually called in and by this time Jock had me whipped away to the M.I. Room (Medical Inspection), where I required five stitches in a head wound and he himself required attention to the shins, where a chair had done some damage. No charges were brought against the revellers, who, by now were hanging round each others necks singing the Canteen 'march past', 'Nellie Dean'.

There were many onlookers lined up on the route to the Station, one of them being Jock Hardy's wife, Ruby, who I did not know at that time. 1940 - Jock was killed in action during the Dunkirk retreat and many years later I was to marry the lady. It's a small world.

We boarded the 'Dilwara' on the evening of the same day and owing to the fact that she was tied up next to the 'Queen Mary', I thought it was one of the life-boats which had accidentally dropped from the davits. The Dilwara was called all sorts of names and none of them complimentary. She was 'Galloping Gerti', 'Roll-a-long' and even 'Kicker'. She was the only ship I know which could dip and roll at one and the same time. I was the only one of my immediate circle of friends who wasn't violently sick, but my word, where others had got it out of their system in a few days, I was to be internally sick for most of the four weeks journey. The food was good and plentiful but on one occasion the desert was rhubarb and custard and the aftermath of this was the inevitable 'runs'. Now the 'Heads' or the toilets were situated at the 'pointed end' of the boat and there were about ten swing door toilets facing each other with a narrow walkway between. The flushing arrangement was a constant running water system coming underneath the seats, and all the individual seats being linked up with the flush way. On this particular day there was a queue awaiting their turn but the occupants were reluctant to move. When my turn came in the queue I entered the toilet at the highest point or the No. 1 toilet. Some of the lads in the waiting queue were getting frantic so I decided to do something about it. I made a torch out of toilet rolls and lit them with a match. I then placed the pyre in boat fashion and placed in the fast flowing water. In no time at all there were ten empty toilets for the boys waiting. There were howls of anguish from the rudely evacuated ex-tenants and I had to get some backing from my mates or I would have joined the Dolphins in the Med.

Some of the 'evacuated' decided that their sex lives would be ruined for all time.

There was a lot of unrest in the Middle East where Mussolini was still huffing and puffing, and after picking up our new Battalion at Haifa, we turned back to Port Said for disembarkation and entrained for Cairo and 'Abbysia' Barracks, there to be detailed off in four groups preparatory to being sent out to Mersa Matru, Moascar and two other places, the names of which escape me. At this time the whole of the British Army were stood to and awaiting Musso's next move after his slaughtering of the unarmed natives of Abbysinia. Incidentally, this was the first and only time that mustard gas was used in action and the pictures of victims presented in the dally press were working the civilised countries up into a wholesale hatred of the users.

We settled down in Abbysia and waited for a couple of weeks and during this time the Draftees put up with the usual banter. "Report to the Quarter Stores for your tropical knees", or "Outside the last Draft to see the aeroplane" or sometimes "Outside the last Draft to see the sandstorm". We were told that where now we had skin like the C.O.'s Charger the 'currant bun' (sun) would soon liken it to the back of our haversacks. A boxing tournament soon took care of the banter when it was noticed that the 'lily whites' were not 'lily livered' and more than held their own with the old sweats.

One of these old timers wanted to know what was the latest song as the 'Lily of Laguna' was all the go when he came out.

During the short stays in some ports we had the usual bum boats and all the characters who were on the look-out for a quick buck at all times. We had the 'gulli' man who had the greatest sleight of hand tricks ever seen. He performed with live chicks all the time chanting "Come chicken, go chicken" at the same time taking a chicken from someone's pocket or from under the topee. He would borrow a watch, put it in a dirty hanky, hit it with a hammer and throw it over the side, much to the consternation of the owner who would have to wait until the magician finished his repertoire before receiving back the undamaged watch. Then we had 'Jock McGreggor' as black as a kettle and selling all sorts of souvenirs. He had a line of patter which claimed "Me Jock McGreggor from Glasgow, left hand side going into Blighty. Many times I walk under Westminster Bridge. God Bless the King. Queen Victoria very good man". He was corrected on the last statement so afterwards he would say "Queen Victoria very good race-horse, two times twice I have seen him"! Another character would row alongside the boat dressed in a loincloth and a magnificent top hat on his head. To go with this ensemble he was always puffing a big cigar. He would ask that we throw silver coins one at a time and he would dive deep down still in top hat and cigar smoking away. When he surfaced he would hold the coin aloft in triumph and the amazing thing about this performance was that the cigar would still be smoking away after being submerged. Many years later I was to read that a shark had beaten this cheerful performer to the punch.

Mussolini must have decided that Libya and Egypt would be too hard a nut to crack and after his so-called 'glorious victories' against the forces of Haile Selassie he decided to call it a day and present himself with a few medals. We were then free to continue our journey to Singapore going by rail from Cairo to port Suez then to rejoin our old friend the Dilwara. We were to go ashore at one more point en route - Ceylon.

We played soccer against the local garrison and in spite of the roaring backing from the rest of our shipmates we were sunk without trace. Owing to the buck jumping antics of the old 'Dilwara' our 'land legs' had deserted us. There appeared to be a lack of co-ordination, but equilibrium became more balanced and equality given a boost at half time when the two sides had a semi-booze up. All light hearted stuff and not likely to hit the back pages. On board again and on the last lap of our journey it was decided to have a boxing tournament solely for the pleasure of the Officers on board. Boxing and brandy made the perfect combination. The outcome of this tournament was to see me reaching the final of my weight only to come a cropper in the final round of the last bout. I was hit so hard by this ex-Wigan miner that I finished up in the second row of the squatting on the deck spectators. I thought the ship had sunk. This lad was as resilient as a rubber ball and later on earned the nick-name of 'Motor-bike' owing to his running abilities, although, I hasten to add, he didn't attempt to run when I fought him. He also had very limited academic qualifications and promotion to Corporal some time later made no improvement. One of his guard reports once quoted 'Orderly Burglar' instead of 'Orderly Bugler'. Nevertheless he was a great lad and especially in a tight corner.

We took over Tanglin Barracks from the Inniskillens, who had moved under canvas awaiting the official take over, but in the meantime the barrack blocks had been taken over by bugs! The first night was a worrying one to say the least, and reveille revealed that every one was outside under the tropical stars. There was a determined attempt to clean out these horrible stinking creatures. Paraffin appeared to be the only deterrent and the place was soon smelling like a garage. The biscuit type mattresses were infested and the only way to clear the eggs was to place the mattresses on ant hills, after first stirring up the residents to make them good and mad.

It took the best part of two weeks to make the place reasonably habitable and even then there was one day a week for 'de-bugging'. A grand ally in this campaign was a Chameleon, which was placed inside the mosquito net and even a Preying Mantis, both of which relished these little pests.

The town of Singapore, or the Lion City, would have been all the better for a similar clean-up because of the scourge of V.D. It was reckoned at the time that one in five of the 'ladies' of the town had the infection. The situation and the high rate of hospital intake became so bad that all victims of this menace automatically forfeited all proficiency pay because of the classification of 'self infliction'. There was also an intercompany competition when the least cases in any one calendar month gave a day's holiday to the lucky lot. Believe me, it was luck. I remember once greeting a friend of mine just being discharged from hospital with the words "Welcome back, you dirty so and so", and receiving the answer "Chuck, there's none more pure than the purified". He could have been right too. Concealment of the condition carried with it the almost certainty of a Court Martial and this usually carried the punishment of 30 days in the "Hotel".

There's no profession more boring than the normal repetitive military training where the emphasis is very much on instinctive re-action to a given situation. I suppose in a way we were robots and the old dogma of "do as I say, not as I do", also "a soldier is not paid to think but to obey without question". We would rise at 6.00 a.m., grab a mug of 'gun fire' (tea) from the buckets placed outside the cookhouse doors by the duty cook. First parade was P.T., followed by a cold shower and then breakfast followed by the inevitable rifle inspection and a bit of arms drill thrown in. These activities ensured some motivation but the boring M.G. (Vickers) routine with the repetition 'pretend' stoppages and remedies. The section would sit in a circle on the verandah whilst the instructor would shout the stoppage for the gun team No. 1 and No. 2 to remedy. The hardest part of this exercise was keeping awake and I was to be in trouble one very hot and humid day. I was a Corporal instructor and the class of ten or so men were going through all the appropriate motions when all of a sudden there was a loud snore! Whether it was envy or the fact that I could bore someone so much or whatever, I don't know, but I got annoyed and told this lad to bring his bedding out of the barrack room at the double. He was then ordered to double round the barrack block three times at the same time carrying his bedding. He ran past the class on two occasions and it was like waiting for the next shoe to drop. I was beginning to think he may have had an accident, like falling asleep on the move and running into a wall. I sent one of the section to look round the end of the building, but at that point the Coy. Segt. Major had decided to have a stroll round his domain. The Sgt. Major sent my messenger back and beckoned me to come instead. There was our marathon running friend, mattresses spread out in the shade, lying flat out, mouth wide open and snoring his head off! At first I feared the worst when I saw him but a bellow from the Sgt. Major had him up on his feet in about two seconds flat! He was 'politely requested' to continue the original punishment with an added bonus of three circuits. The Sgt. Major gave me a 'dressing down' but the twinkle in his eye took the sting out of his words and I had the greatest difficulty keeping my face straight, especially when the victim came round on his first circuit and whilst passing behind the Sgt. Major made an obscene gesture towards him.

If there had been no sporting activities I think we should have gone round the bend. Even the outbreak of war in Europe had little effect on our lives for quite some time, except for the feverish rush to set up beach defences of timber framing and dannet wire. This defence line was set up in the tide itself and backed up by sawn trees which were let into the ground for five feet and angled towards the sea. This was apparently to stop marine craft getting a foothold on the beach. Every 800 yds there were concrete 'pill boxes' to hold two gun teams each with a search light. It's a pity the Japs made no attempt to land on this coast but chose the soft belly West side of the Island which had no or little defenses. Anyhow, I'm way ahead of my story because at this time the Japs were waiting the outcome of the European conflict before making their take-over bid of British possessions in the Far East. They would no more like the Germans in that sphere than the British.

Physical fitness was the priority, and one Sandhurst type in my Company thought up a toughening up exercise. The No. 2 Sports ground was set in a valley and comprised of two soccer fields and a hockey field. Dividing each of the playing fields there ran a Malarial drain, each side about 10' back from the touch line. All the Company of about 200 men were numbered off into two teams making 100 a side, dressed in K.D. shorts, socks and ammunition boots, bare from the waist up. The teams were lined up facing each other on the centre of the hockey field. From a safe vantage point the Officer gave a soccer ball a 'Rugger' kick into the middle. There were no rules as such, except that the action ceased on the blowing of a whistle. The idea was to get the ball through the opponents goal posts by any means possible, kicking, shoving, thumping or biting. Everything was legal! The place was littered with bodies both in and out of the four feet deep concrete malarial drains. Old scores were settled; most times the game just developed into a free for all and no thought given to the ball. This was to be the first time I heard a shouted order "Never mind the ball, get on with the game"! The Medical Officer soon put paid to this game when he was inundated with dozens of fractures and lacerations. He even suggested that the ball should be replaced by the Officer who thought up the game!

When the Jap forces invaded Indo China each Platoon was paraded outside the Barrack block and 'let into the picture' by the Platoon Sergeants who had already been primed by the Battalion Adjutant. We had a real one! First of all he said "Well, lads the balloon as gone hup!". One or two of us scanned the sky above his head and he told us not to be 'Higerant'! He went on "First of all I must tell you the Japs are coming through Hindigo China, and not only that, they are using higerant hanimals". The reference was to the Guerrilla tactics used by the Jap forces. He meant well and the message sank in. The Canteens were really swinging that night and the thought of action was exhilarating, but had we known what was to follow there would have been more mourning than celebrating.

Part II

Playtime

The year 1941. The month November and the place: Singapore, already feeling the hot blast of war from the yellow hordes of His Imperial Highness Emperor Hirioto. My unit had been stationed in Tanglin Barracks from the end of 1938 and most of us were accustomed to the hot tropical suns and frequent thunder storms which swept over the Island from Sumatra. The normal training activities usually ceased around mid-day when the heat got a little uncomfortable. After cold showers and lunch the old soldier rule of 'in bed or out of barracks' came into effect and woe betide any 'rookie' who stepped out of line during this 2 to 4 period. After tea the inter-company sporting activities took over - football, rugby, hockey, cricket etc., sometimes there was a battalion match against the 'Gordons', the 'Argylles', the 'R.E.'s' or possibly the 'R.A.F.' who considered themselves a cut above the old 'Squaddies'. They were known as the 'Brylcream Boys' or the 'Pamphlet Droppers', in those days and our battalion team, sometimes known as 'Canteen Eleven' were advised by the partisan crowd to 'bring them down in flames' and other rude and unprintable remarks. Weekends were usually spent down the 'pore, first the Union Jack Club on Orchard Road, before heading for the 'New World' or the 'Great World' Cabarets. Whiskey was about two Straits dollars a bottle and Tiger beer around 20 cents a bottle, so with the Straits dollar around 2/4 the cost of inebriation was low. Rickshaw pullers were very easily egged on to race one against the other and many were the racing spills on Orchard Road with the 'merry' passengers finishing up in the 'malar-

56

ial drains'. Life was just one round of training, sport, supping up and womanising. But all this was soon to come to an end with the bombing of Pearl Harbour and incidentally, the bombing of Singapore Island on the same night - December 7th 1941! Anyhow, all this is getting ahead of my story which starts in Tanglin Barracks with a call to the R.S.M.'s office with the somewhat peculiar instruction to myself to pick a team of four who could be relied upon to handle a 'Tommy Gun' and be prepared to use it if called upon. The selection was left to myself and quite naturally I handed in to the R.S.M. a list of six men, of my own platoon, leaving the final selection to him.

The instruction was to rendezvous at the entrance to the Botanical Gardens and there to be picked up by an Officer of the Pay Corps at 10.00 a.m. We were bang on time, not wanting to be so conspicuous standing around fully armed. Eventually the pick up was made by a 30 cwt Army truck. Remember, all this time we had no idea of knowing the nature of our mission but in those days it was a case of 'do as I say' without questions.

On boarding the truck we proceeded up the Buckit Timah Road and in due course arrived at the entrance to the Seletar Naval Base, where, after some paper checking, we were allowed to enter, albeit still under the scrutiny of the Naval guards who didn't appear to be very happy about the automatic weapons we carried. On reaching the quayside I was instructed by the Pay Officer to fan my men out around the truck facing away, and it then dawned on me the reason for all the secrecy, when naval ratings started humping ammunition boxes down the gangway from the *Repulse* and stacking them in our truck. Our Officer in charge then took me into his confidence with the information that the boxes contained Treasury Bullion which had been cleared from the 'Hong Kong' and 'Shanghai' Banks in Hong Kong and was to be transferred to the sister Bank in Singapore. He confided that there was probably £2,000,000 and the strictest secrecy had to be maintained then, and after the mission had been accomplished. My instructions on pulling out from the Naval Base was to set my men facing out from the tail-board of the truck and one in the front seat. The 'pans' had to be affixed to the automatics ready for instant action if approached in any way by another vehicle or in the possible event of an ambush en route. By this time I had passed all the information on to my four comrades and I sensed they were just hoping we would be 'jumped' on the long road to

Singapore. However we arrived in Raffles Square without incident and surrounded the truck at the Bank entrance until the consignment had to be signed over to the Bank authorities. It was something of an anti-climax when the responsibility had been transferred and the 'Tommy' guns assumed the garb of peashooters, leaving us with the feeling that we had been cheated out of a bit of action. On being dropped off at our original rendezvous I was given the magnificent amount of ten Dollars to share out with my men. This was classified as a missed meal allowance and had to be signed for. Ten Dollars for riding shot-gun on £2,000,000! How's that for comparison? The ten Dollars was put on the table in the men's wet canteen and although we had a good session on the Tiger beer, it tasted rather flat to me. Although the war had raged since 1939 we in Singapore still lived in peacetime conditions but this was soon to end and we were to get more action than we bargained for, starting with the Battalion dispersal to the Beach defences, my own Company being positioned on the East Coast and my section on Betin Kusah Point.

Action

Betin Kusah 'Pill-box' became something of a prison to my fed up mates and myself after weeks of 'stand to' and 'stand down'. We began to hate the place with its surrounding swamps and a breeding place for millions of mosquitoes which necessitated the use of Warzeristan cream to be smeared on faces and hands. I can hear those damned 'quitoes even now with their amazing aptitude for dive-bombing and latching on to unprotected flesh and drawing on your life blood. Unofficially we had a few bottles of whiskey buried for tea-lacing but once in a while the whole bottles were emptied and we were very merry warriors indeed on being picked up on some occasions.

The Pill Boxes were linked up by field telephone and controlled from the Coy H.Q. where a Lieut. was in command. He was responsible for our only activity of 'stand to' and 'stand down' at Sunset and Dawn. There were many variations of this order barked out over the 'phone to all Pill Box commanders. On one memorable occasion we were ordered to "man the palisades, Buffalo Bill is riding by"! and another time we were instructed by the 'phone orderly to "stand to, socks bandolier fashion, shirts at halfmast"! There were also many variations on the reply to these commands and they weren't so mild as 'get stuffed'. We were occasionally billeted in the Selarang Barracks at this time, as the 'Gordons' had been transferred to the mainland and held in reserve whilst our forces were making a series of 'tactical withdrawals' down the Malay Peninsular. There was a leave rota which allowed us down Singapore for four hours at a time and a threat that any returnees under the influence would be placed in the 'Kunji' where the Crows won't shit on you", or words to that effect. There was also the cunning system of breaking up known mates and not allowing them leave at the same time. One occasion will always be remembered by me when, accompanied by Sam Gledhill, we made our way to the U.J. Club on Orchard Road and started on the Tiger beer with the occasional whiskey thrown in. The place was full of 'Argylles', 'Surreys', 'Leicesters' and many more representatives from the Loyals, R.E.'s etc., all out to enjoy a short life but a merry one. Most of the Argylles (Gargoyles) were just out of hospital after wounds sustained in the northern part of the country, and made no secret of the fact that they weren't very friendly disposed towards my unit, who were classified as Fortress Command, only to be used in our official capacity of Vickers machine gunners and to man the Pill boxes spread out down the East Coast from Bedoh Point to Betin Kusah. Many were the jibes of 'never been off the Island' and many were the free for alls which usually accompanied these remarks. On the particular day that Gledhill and I were there, we decided to take off and try to reach the forward troops who were at that time just south of Ipoh. The combination of the beer and the added insults must have put fire in our bellies which set us off on this wild venture. We made our way to the Station after a bit of dodging about through the back alleys of the old Chinatown, there to intermingle with an Indian Army unit ,who were being rushed overnight to try and stem the Japs, who were pushing down from just north of Ipoh, after inflicting heavy casualties on the 'Leicesters', 'Surreys' and 'Argyles'. These units took the first brunt of the initial attack, and were mauled to the extent of having the formation of the 'Surrey/Leicesters' to be known as the British Battalion. Our aim was to report to the H.Q. of this Bn. and volunteer for any front line post they would allocate.

On the overnight journey up through the jungles and plains of Malaya we decided to await our chance and jump off the train just south of Kuala Lumpar - if the train should slow down. In fact, we didn't have to jump off the moving train as it steamed to a halt in a siding just a few miles short of K.L. Leaving the train was not without its excitement as we had to dodge a couple of vigilant 'Red Caps', who were on duty in this particular Kampong. A couple of our late train companions also decided to have a shot at us but with a bit of jinking and weaving we were able to make the thick jungle to the side of the main road. The Red Caps gave it up as a lost cause, thus allowing us to relax a while with a fag and a chance to work out our next move. By now, we were cold, sober and very hungry. We were also very apprehensive about our chance of reaching the British Battalion alive because by now a hue and cry would be raised, and in fact, we heard afterwards, that we had to be taken dead or alive because of the chance we may be members of the so-called Fifth Column, who were reputed to be operating in this area. The Fifth Column were members of various spy rings and were everywhere. We spent most of that day just lying low and watching the coming and going of Military traffic. Come dusk we decided to chance trying to reach K.L. and mingle with the troops already there, working on the principle of safety in numbers. We had amazing luck and even managed to purchase a feed of 'Nasi Goreng' from one of the native street vendors. I never tasted anything so good even though by that time the rain was bucketing down as it only can in the Tropics. The next problem was to find a place to 'doss' down for the night but we soon overcome this by finding an old disused storehouse which was reasonably dry. The excitement of the day must have exhausted us because the next thing we knew was the sound of the early risers clearing the throats and spitting betel nuts all over the place. We used to refer to this noise as the 'Indian Love Call'. From here we made our way through the half empty streets to the main road heading north, and set off along the highway with no pretence of hiding. After an hour's trudging in the hot sun we heard a lorry coming up the road behind us and the chatter of many voices, in fact there were two lorries and both loaded up with un-armed soldiers. We decided to wave them down to try and bluff our way but there was no need because we were invited to climb aboard and travel with them. We were informed that they were the remnants of Leics. and Surreys who had been cut off during heavy fighting to the North but had got out of the bag by taking to the sea and travelled down to the coast by anything floatable. When they considered they were out of the danger area they had struck for the beach and after commandeering a couple of native lorries were on their way to rejoin their units which, by this time, was known as the British Battalion.

Kampar

A couple of hours travel brought us into the battle area which was at that time a line from Tanjong Malim to the west, and the jungle slopes over the River Kampar, with a fairly clear view of the Plains south of Ipoh. Our own 25lb Batteries were pounding away and retaliatory mortars and howitzers were dropping uncomfortably close when we were told to dis-embus and form up under cover of the rubber trees until identification and dispersals were completed. The R.S.M. didn't know how to handle the situation of we two cuckoos in the nest and was even suspicious of our AB 64's which we carried on our person. During this interrogation we were under the pointed rifles of two of the H.Q. signallers and we got the impression they were looking forward to the chance of giving us some lead sandwiches. First the Adjutant was called to sort it out and then Lt. Col. Johnston took over.

We were locked up in an old attap roofed hut still under armed guard whilst attempts were made to contact our unit in Singapore, the H.Q. at that time being up the Changi Road opposite Nee Soon village.

All this time we were under mortar fire and the air was filled with dust and bits from the surrounding rubber trees. We were extremely jumpy and expecting the next noisy arrival to be all ours. After what seemed hours we were led out to the slit trench occupied by the C.O. and Adjutant. Contact had been made with our Bn. H.Q. and positive identity determined. We were given a good dressing down by the Col. and then told we would be given something to eat and put into a forward Vickers machine gun position. By this time night had fallen and our guide was a bundle of nerves having to go forward and find the slit trench emplacement which was now under constant fire. His nerves held out until just about 50 yds from the manned position which he pointed out to us, or rather the direction of the position, and then scarpered back to H.Q.

I remember the pass word being 'Alor Star' but even so the approach to the position was very dodgy indeed because these chaps had been under constant fire for weeks on end and any noise by us before getting within whispering range could be our last move. However being old sweats, adept in the art of making use of ground and cover we managed this tricky manoeuvre even to the extent of whispering the pass word 'Alor Star' into the ear of what proved to be the Cpl in charge. He very nearly took off through his tin helmet but after an hysterical laugh he settled down and took command of the situation. We were then led forward to an even more forward position and relieved two chaps who had a Vickers set up on the forward buttress of a slit trench. Relieved is an understatement. They were delighted!

When we appraised the position at dawn, and after a night of constant bombardment, we could understand why.

First of all we were on the forward slope of a hill looking down into a rather steep valley, with plenty of small bush clumps on the way, and bounded on the right by a mountainous range of jungle. The hill, in fact was a Chinese cemetery and as the old macabre joke of the 'dead centre' came to me I hoped it wasn't going to have any bearing on Gledhill and myself. We were relieved from our post around mid morning and after the heavy rains of the night before the sun was steaming the surrounding vegetation. Fires were not allowed in this vulnerable position so we had to make do with cold tinned bacon and water from the waterbottles. Gledhill and I didn't even have a water bottle between us, but we all mucked in. We were just relaxing with a fag after this great meal when a terrific hubbub started just over the crest of the hill 20 yds away, screaming and banging all over the place. Grabbing a rifle apiece we went forward to see Japs attempting a takeover of our position. One had hold of our Vickers gun and was trying to dislodge it from its mounting, when he saw us coming in fast with the bayonet. He decided that discretion was the better part of valour and dived headlong from the gun before rolling down the steep slope. There were only about ten of us in this skirmish and only one casualty sustained by our lot when one of the lads had a bullet through the knee. The Cpl in charge of our small team was awarded the M.M. for showing aggression and fighting off this determined attack by a large fighting patrol of Japs.

Counter Attack

Later on in the day we were told that a Bn. of Sikhs and one of Punjabis were going into a counter attack at 2.00 p.m. The three gun positions in our overlooking area were to lay down a zone of fire on to a small hillock immediately to our front, as information had filtered back that there was a build up of some strength just beyond. At 1.57 on a synchronised watch check we started blazing away sights set 500 yds. We were amazed at the activity on this small hill, where up to now, there had been no movement. Enemy troops were lifting like a covey of partridge, and some 'hitting the deck' as smartly as they lifted. Our concentrated fire must have taken them completely by surprise, and their only aim was to get out of this hot spot and behind the cover of the hill. My mate, Gledhill, was whooping as he fed the belts into the gun and shouting "another bastard. and another! - Whee!". He was trying to speed up the intake of the belt by pushing and we were dead lucky that he didn't cause a double-feed stoppage.

On exactly 2.00 p.m. the Cpl in charge hit me on the shoulder to stop firing. After this excitement and noise there was a deathly hush until the Sikhs and Punjabis started going in with yells and screams, which could be plainly heard from our positions. The sun was gleaming on bayonets and the swords of the British Officers who led the charge. As the Indian troops rushed in the Japs came forward and there was a right old ding-dong going in our full view with Jap Officers swinging their two handed Samurai swords. This battle lasted for about 15 minutes, when the Indian line broke and pulled back in disorder to the screams of "Banzai! Banzai!" from the Japs. The Indians must have given them a right old mauling before pulling back, because only a half hearted attempt was made to follow up by the Japs. After this attack everything settled down to the normal mortar bombarding and we were so accustomed to this that we knew when to duck by the sound of the approaching shells. The duds had a loose whirring sound and I have heard it said that you never hear the one with your number on it. Who's to prove or disprove this theory? The dead don't talk! Our own 25lb'ers were looping shells over our heads and trying to pinpoint the Japs to our front and they were getting great service in this activity by an R.A. Officer, who had an O.P. (Observation Point) just a few yards from our gun position. We were sorry to see him retire to his battery that day because he was spot on and even managed to hit a Jap armoured car, which had nosed its way around a bend in the main road about 400 yards to our left. Whether the wheels had been blown off or not I don't know, but an effective road block had been determined by just one shot and later a barrage just beyond to dispel any further attempts to break through. It hadn't registered with us up to that time that this was New Year's Day 1941, until an orderly crawled up from H.Q. with a packet of fags per man, a gallon of water and a sarcastic 'Happy New Year' greeting - Bloody Hell Later on that day was the time I actually looked death in the face and but for natural animal instincts I would have had no further interest in the war.

Sam had been sent to rejoin H.Q. as the C.O.'s runner and a replacement, Paddy Slaney, joined me. I can see Paddy's homely 'mush' now, happy go lucky and entirely fearless. It was a very hot day and we decided to spell each other off and try and catch up with a 'kip' down. On the toss of a coin I had first rest whilst Paddy 'stood to' armed with a 'Tommy' gun and just looking over the slit trench alongside the Vickers. I had hardly stretched out on the rear side of the trench when every sense in me came alive. Looking me in the face from about two yards in front of the Vickers was a Jap, his helmet festooned with foliage and looking ready to pounce on Paddy, who I suspected of being asleep. I hurled myself across the trench and grabbed the Vickers handgrips, just as the Jap turned tail and dived back into the shrubbery. Everything happened at once, Paddy blasted off with the automatic while I pressed the thumb piece of the bigger gun at the same time, swinging in an arc directed at the point of retreat taken by the Jap scout. There was no return fire or movement of any sort, and after a while I decided to have a 'shufti' to the immediate front because I felt sure one of us had hit the enemy at that range. I snake crawled forward for about 20 yds and had a good look round but nobody. On my way back I put out my hand to pull aside some shrubbery and felt the slimy feel of blood. There was quite a lot on the bushes and one or two flattened down grass patches denoting that boyo had not been alone. After being hit he must have been dragged back down the hill by his comrades. From then on it was full alert and another two lads were sent to join us with instructions that we were there to stay, come what may. At dusk it was decided to send out a recce patrol of six men and although I volunteered (to relieve the boredom I might add) I was told to stay put behind the Vickers as I was the only qualified gunner at that time, and in that place. The patrol eventually returned from the pre-determined direction and reported enemy build up activity to our front and more alarming still on our right flank and partial rear through a gully. The 25lb'ers had pulled out by this time and we all knew what this meant -

another tactical withdrawal.

Withdrawal

Just before midnight and with the moon coming up over the jungle heights to our right, we were ordered to prepare to withdraw as quietly as possible and make our way back to H.Q. on the main road. The two Bren gun positions had to go first and after 10 minutes it was our turn. This was the longest 10 minutes of my life when imagination ran riot and every bush was the 'hideout' of the Imperial Nipponese Army.

Eventually our turn came and the gun was dismantled as quietly as possible. Our problem was now to hump the tripod and gun down to our supply rear and also six boxes of belted ammunition. Reluctantly, we realised that it would take a return journey to pick up the four belt boxes still on the slit trench position. The return journey was eerie and the now bright moonlight made it even more hazardous with not knowing what to expect every step of the way up that hill. Quite frankly I was amazed that the Japs had allowed all this moving about and doing nothing about it.

We were two very happy squaddies when we finally arrived back at the rendezvous for the big exodus and even more chuffed when we were presented with a bottle of sherry sent to us by the C.O. for the 'two Chesters' (Manchesters). He was obviously pleased with our first turn out for his 'Mob'. We just managed to get all our gear on one of a long line of R.A.S.C. trucks when heavy firing opened up from the hill just recently vacated by ourselves.

We were being plastered with the heavy mortar fire not only from our recent positions but from the other flank as well. It seemed like the enemy had infiltrated down the coast and also made landings on the beach itself some 20 miles west of Kampar. They must have been in great strength as indicated by the heavy and determined volume of small arms and mortar fire. We had about 30 lorries lined up on the road ready for a quick withdrawalbut the net was closing quickly. Already five or six lorries had been put out of action by the deadly accurate mortars. In the midst of all this bedlam the Colonel decided to risk a quick load up with everything we could salvage by way of guns, ammunition etc. and try and break through the rapidly closing bottle neck of our escape route. The damaged lorries had been manhandled off the road by now and just unceremoniously tipped into the deep ditches each side of the main 'drag'. We all clambered aboard the remaining wagons after first making sure that our wounded were gathered together and allocated the three central lorries in the convoy. We were on the move, but not for long. The sudden stop of vehicles and total black out conditions plus the ensuing noise resembled a railway shunting yard, but fortunately the slow advance did very little damage, excepting a chap in my lorry, who had been dangling his legs over the tail end. His leg was badly shattered and later on had to be amputated. The sudden stop of the convoy had been caused by a couple of fallen trees lying across the road and inspection indicated that they had been deliberately chopped through and not just the result of heavy fire. A fighting patrol of 50 men was sent forward with fixed bayonets and very shortly afterwards the sounds of close combat could be heard. There was a lot of screaming and shouting of orders for about 10 minutes when all went quiet. Of the 50 men who had been sent forward only 30 survived but they had broken through the road block of banked up trees and a determined force of Japanese who, though outnumbered put up a very strong fight and fought to the last man. The convoy then moved on past this gory encounter and once on the move the firing quickly diminished to our rear.

After about 3 hours travel we pulled into a rubber plantation and were ordered to dis-embus. A brew of tea and 'corned-dog' sandwiches were already waiting for us on arrival and these were devoured in a matter of seconds, but for me the hot sweet tea made my day/night. We were told to get our heads down after some unlucky lads had been detailed for perimeter 'stand to'. I had no groundsheet to spread on the wet ground but managed to rake together some dead leaves and after removing the boots from sore and blistered feet was soon in the arms of Morpheus.

Knock Out

I was very soon to be sharply and painfully wakened when a 30 cwt lorry stopped on my legs, not across but from ankles to knees. The pain was excruciating and the rude awakening was accompanied by the nightmare that the vehicle was a Jap tank. It was a miracle how the lorry stopped and I can only owe my life to the fact that I was stretched out with my head resting against a tree. It was this which stopped the driver, when shown up in his 'black-out' slit lights. One of the Surrey's lying next to me was on his feet and threatening to shoot the poor shocked driver before they eventually heaved the lorry front wheel off my tortured legs. After the initial pain all feeling left my legs and this condition was to remain with me for about a week. I was heaved into the same truck, incidentally, and taken down to a forward Ambulance station at Tanjong Malim, where I was trussed up like a chicken before being transported further down the line to a hospital in Kuala Lumpar. This travelling took up all the day and my only recollection is the sight of a medical orderly wearing a blood stained apron and looking completely exhausted. I woke up in a bed, clean and dressed in a sarong but can't remember much about this as complete exhaustion had taken over and to me the Malay and Chinese nurses were angels floating around in white smocks, God bless them!

A few hours later saw the evacuation of the hospital, when the Japs intensified the bombing from the air and were getting dangerously close on the ground. The Red Cross marked train was packed with serious and walking wounded and after a lot of huffing and puffing we were under way, the British R.E. driver and mate at the controls, the native drivers having found safer jobs. We were to run the gauntlet of overhead planes on a couple of occasions but whether the Jap pilots had run out of ammunition or assumed the mantle of Knights in shining armour I wouldn't know but we were allowed to continue 'unbombed'.

Late evening found us being off-loaded on to ambulances and taken to the General Hospital in Johore Baruh right next to the Sultan's Palace. The ten days spent in there was a far cry from the chaos, muck and flying lead of the few days previous. The staff were marvellous and kept their cool even when handling the most severe wounded being admitted daily.

Loss At Sea

Whilst I was in this haven there was a sudden flurry of activity and sailor clad figures started trickling in from the sunken 'Prince of Wales' and 'The Repulse'. This was a desperate blow to our morale and I consider the most stupid tactics ever carried out by the British Navy in foreign waters completely covered by the not inconsiderable strength of the Nippon Air Force. They had already proved their determination and strength when the eagle was bearded in his eyrie at Pearl Harbour. History has proved that these two mighty warships weren't mighty enough and were completely thrown away with heavy loss of life and a kick in the guts of every serviceman in the Pacific.

My legs were still decidedly puffy when discharged on 15th January 1942, but much of the numb feeling had left them and I was able to get around albeit a little slowly. From the hospital we were taken to what was known as a M.R.C. (mixed Reinforcement Camp) and here was the odds and sods of every unit in Malaya, ex-wounded, ex-sick or whatever. The idea was to try and get intakes back to fighting condition and then return to their own units or possibly to rush to some hard pressed sector. However, I was sent back to my own unit, the Bn. H.Q. at that time being at the 11th Kilo milestone Changi Road. I wasn't exactly welcomed with open arms, being placed in close custody - again! I was only in the cooler about one hour when Gledhill was thrown in and don't ask me how he managed that because the last time I had seen him we were under fire at Kampar. The following day we were wheeled in front of the C.O. Col. E.B. Holmes (Manchester Reg.). He roasted us in no uncertain fashion and then decided that we should have a Field General Court Martial for 'Desertion in the face of the enemy' - I ask you! We absconded from the comparative peace of the Singapore East Coast and reported for killing duties in the front line!! Found guilty on this charge in the field could mean facing a firing squad and I don't try to hide the fact that we weren't very happy about this. Anyhow, the following day saw us marched in front of the 'old man' again and I detected a change in his attitude. Although he explained that only organised resistance would beat the enemy he actually said he was pleased with our conduct whilst being with the British Bn. and had a letter from Col. Johnston asking for leniency. The Col. also stated that we were good senior N.C.O. material and would be accepted by his unit any time. We were given an instant dismissal by Col. Holmes and told to rejoin our Company. Back to where we started. Betin Kusah pill box.

Backs To The Sea

Towards the end of January 1942 our troops having withdrawn over the Johore Causeway and a half hearted attempt made to blow this structure to smithereens, we were ordered to withdraw from the outer positions as we were in danger of a classical 'cut off'. Around midnight on the last day of January we pulled back on to the Changi Road on a crossing known to us as the 'Laundry Cross-roads' and there ordered to set up a position to cover the withdrawal of the R.A. who were setting up the explosives in the 15" Batteries. Around 1.00 a.m. there was the most awful explosion and we could hear bits and pieces flying through the air all round us and then a deathly quiet. My two gun positions were just 1/4 mile from the main road and facing up a small secondary road, running parallel with the main 'drag'. We were told that anything moving on this road would be of enemy origin, and we were to open up with everything we had. It was a real spooky situation until we heard the sound of marching feet coming from the so-called enemy territory and everything ready for the big blast off, but the situation being what it was, chaotic and confused, we held our fire until we could be sure that we weren't going to mow down our own troops. With incredible bravery, one of our lads Joe Mitchell (known as the 'Shuffling King-pin' because of his prowess in the ring) elected to go forward to meet the marching column, identify and signal back to us by means of a hand torch. A circular swing with the torch meant we had to give him a few seconds to dive for cover and then open up with our two Vickers. A flat left to right signal meant not to fire as it could be assumed that the marching column were our own troops. It was a hair raising 5 minutes I can tell you, but eventually we got the 'flat' signal not to fire and then Joe hove in sight at the head of a platoon of Gurkhas, who had been cut off in the earlier fighting, and were making their way back to join up with their own unit. How in Heaven Joe knew the difference between Johnny Gurkha and the Japs was a mystery to me, especially in the dark. This was one occasion where the old Army rule of 'do without question' proved to be a stupid misnomer. The withdrawal from this point proved to be uneventful and the big white chiefs having decreed that a last stand defensive perimeter be set up around the City itself, we very soon found ourselves all together as a Coy. (D), the Coy. Commdr. being Capt. Stewart or 'Horsey Stewart'. We had ample time to prepare our defensive positions with eight Vickers M.G.'s and numerous Bren guns between each gun replacement around the outskirts of Paya Lebah village. The whole area was rice paddy fields and to step off the in-between tracks meant being up to the knees in squelchy water and mud.

By this time the Jap or Nippon forces had made a break through on the West Coast through the Jurong Marshes and various units had fanned out across the Island and were closing in fast. We just came under sporadic small arms fire after two days.

On one occasion I was standing upright whilst 'Wiley' Watkins, a staunch self-preservationist, was making use of ground and cover, lying on his stomach and for some reason known only to the Jap sniper, 'Wiley' became the target. He was hit twice in the thigh with 28 mm calibre bullets and I had to drag him out of the assumed line of fire. Why did the Nip pick on poor old 'Wiley' and not the more obvious target - myself? Old 'Dad' Middleton got picked off that day and Joe Mitchell once again showed a lot of courage by trying to fish him out of the paddy and drag him back but had to give up the idea when 'Dad' died and slid under the water. By this time the firing had intensified and we were in grave danger of being encircled with all our equipment. The order was given to prepare to pull back on to the main road at 8.00 p.m. under cover of darkness. One gun at a time was taken out and by 9.00 p.m. we were all set in a new position covering three approach roads on the edge of the village, an attack being expected from any one of the three roads. We put in a very uneasy night with everyone on the alert sitting in position behind the guns. A patrol was sent out around midnight. No contact was made with the enemy but they left us in no doubt that they were there by shouting from the surrounding jungle and swamp. They were mouthing "I'm coming to get you, Johnny!" in a very high pitched tone of voice and there must have been an English speaking squad detailed to this task. We just lay low and waited with itchy fingers until the dawn when a barrage of mortars started dropping around us. My section were in position across the road from the jungle, but were obscured somewhat by high bushes on the edge of the jungle.

There was a long concrete malarial drain running from between the two M.G.'s and under the road away from the position to our front. I volunteered to take up position in front of the guns behind a large tree on the edge of the concrete drain, note any enemy movement, give fire directions, and get the hell out of it, into the drain and back under the road to the two guns. By now we were getting well and truly clobbered with mortars and to make matters worse our own artillery started dropping short, boxing us between enemy and 'friendly' fire. The Japs systematically started picking off one gun after another starting at the furthest point from our Section or so I thought! I was shouting fire directions and nipping down into the drain between bouts of fire, thinking I was dead clever, but I was to get a rude reminder that there was a war on. I had just clambered up the drain and behind 'my' tree when everything turned upside down, flashing lights and blackness engulfed me. I came to and started feeling for my limbs. Everything appeared to be intact excepting a lot of blood from my thighs, half of my head appeared to be missing, and I was bleeding from nose and ear. My Section Commander Tommy Cunliffe scrambled under the road to drag me through the shallow water in the drain. It was quite some time before I could take stock of my injuries which proved to be superficial with concrete chippings from the drain embedded in my legs, and what appeared to be a burst ear drum which was giving me hell. The tree had been giving me cover during this action but had been directly hit about two foot above my head and on the other side away from me. It was now lying across the road making an effective road block if the Japs were to attempt a dash through with their armoured cars. Everything became somewhat confused to me from that point on, but I remember we pulled back once again to a point about a mile down the main road on the way to the City and once again the remaining Five guns were placed in position only this time we were informed that the 'Punjabis' were on our right and the 'Dogras' on the left forming a solid line of resistance. Some line of resistance! Patrols were sent out to try and make contact with the Indian troops on each flank but no dice! We were sticking out like a sore thumb straddling the main road but wide open on the flanks which the Japs soon found out. After another uneasy day and night we were pretty exhausted and existing on the odd 'bully' sandwiches washed down with precious water from our water bottles.

Where's The Rugby Team?

Came the dawn once again and all hell broke loose to our rear. We were being hammered with mortars plus heavy and light M.G. fire and once again our own '9 mile snipers' who had once again assumed that our position had been over-run. We were really pinned down for a couple of hours and by this time had been joined by a mixed bunch of Indians, Malay Volunteers, some of whom had wounds but still mobile. We had two old lorries, the flat bottom 30 cwt type with side and tail boards and a move was made to get all our guns, ammunitions etc. aboard. 'Durzy' Taylor and another tough guy 'Jacko' decided to mount fully loaded guns on each side of the first lorry and blast through in the true John Wayne fashion. When everything was ready the word 'go' was given by 'Horsey' Stewart with the most unusual words shouted out above the gun fire "Where's the rugby team? fix bayonets and cha-a-a-rage". This was the first time I had been in this position but the feeling was one of exhilaration only and no sense of fear whatever. It wasn't until afterwards I realised I was going in holding my 'Tommy' gun in true bayonet fighting manner. I could see men dropping on every side but the excitement had really gripped us and I think at that time we were all screaming lunatics. During these few minutes lorries took off down the road to freedom with the Coy. Cmmdr. on board and the two 'John Waynes' blasting the jungle each side of the road. Heavy casualties forced us to stop this suicidal charge and we dropped where we were to re-coup our losses and try and plan our next move. In all we lost about 30 men in this encounter, most being Indians and 'Volunteers'. We found a few wounded lying about and tried to do what we could to fix them up. The aftermath of this skirmish was to be the first time ever I have seen British troops gathered together in a council of war and the young officer in charge to ask the opinion of we 'old sweats' as to our form of action from there. It was decided to strike off in a westerly direction to try to outflank the enemy who just appeared to be holding the ground each side of the main road. The decision was also taken to carry our wounded so it was hard work for the survivors (maybe 25 in all). After an hour's slog through the jungle, the swamp and the bamboo we eventually arrived on the secondary road running from the Bididari Cemetery to the Geylang Road. There was a battery of R.A. in position here and we were lucky not to be mown down when breaking out of the jungle as these chaps were very jumpy indeed. Besides manning their guns they were well armed with small arms weapons. Something happened here which will live with me until I die. Joe Mitchell (The Shuffling Kingpin) decided that it was undignified for a British soldier to be chased by the 'little rickshaw pullers' as he called the Japs, so decided to go back to 'sort 'em out', first of all asking if I would accompany him as we were the only two with sub-machine guns. I couldn't convince him that the move was stupid and that our chance would come later when they really closed in. However nothing would deter him and having said he would 'sort 'em out' he went back into the jungle in the general direction of our late adversaries. Joe was never heard of or seen again, but of one thing I am sure, he would go down with gun blazing, such was the sheer aggression of the man. The officer in charge of our small band was awarded the M.C. but all Joe got was a muddy grave, if that. I think we all realised that the end was near and all the talk of huge reinforcements and air support was a load of bull. The Jap planes by now were zooming in by the hundreds, unchallenged and arrogant. Their Naval units were lobbing shells into the City and they had heavy artillery bombarding from the outer perimeter. An off-shore island known to us as Shell Island was throwing up huge columns of black smoke presumably having been given the 'scorched earth' treatment and at this time some of our so-called Malay friends were sniping from the rear. We made our way down the Geyland Road and on the way rooted two snipers out of one building, both Malays.

We were amazed to meet a platoon of British O/R's who were marching in step with a Sgt. calling out the step! They were all in very clean K.D. and rifles were slung in the proper route march fashion. We were mud splattered, filthy and unshaven and the contrast was startling. We stopped them and enquired who they were to which the Sergeant replied "The Recce Corps - 18th Div.". We had never heard of such a unit or division at that time but one of our lads pointed out that if they carried on in the direction they were heading they would be known as the 'Wreckage Corps', as there was no-one in front other than the enemy. This information appeared to satisfy them and they considered their mission was accomplished so the about turn command by the Sgt. soon had them heading in the other direction.

Our officer in charge decided that a return to H.Q. was the best move, there to re-group and come under direct battle orders, rather than wander round as a small mixed up group. We said good-bye to our Indian and Volunteer friends and set off to find our Unit H.Q. which at that time was on Temple Road. The R.S.M. was still very 'parade ground' and we were ordered to get shaved and cleaned up in general, reporting back to him within the hour! I suppose he thought it was good for morale and no doubt he was right. This was the fateful 15th February, 1942. The day when General Percival and Shenton-Thomas (The Island Governor) decided to call it a day owing to heavy civilian casualties. The Island's supply of water came from one reservoir which was now in the hands of the Japs and we were completely encircled. The order was passed round to lay down our arms at 8.00 p.m. When I joined the Army in 1933, I would never have thought to hear such a command! We were bewildered, sick and angry and this feeling stayed with us for the next 3¹/₂ years of incarceration in the inhuman prison camps. We considered we had given our all with little backing from our country's government at that time. You don't win wars with no air support and this was to be proved time and again.

They pushed us back to Singapore,
From Keddah to Colliers's Quay,
And I would that my mouth would utter,
The thoughts that arise in me,
So that I could tell the story
Of the brave stand that *never* was made,
By the Army that *never* was beaten,
But the Army that was betrayed.

Now here we sit, indurance vile,
Held thrall in a foreign land,
Not knowing whether to laugh or cry,
At the 'Malayan High Command'.

Banzai

At 8.00 p.m. (20.00 hrs) the big silence set in after the firing ceased although the odd small arms shot here and there indicated that human life was still being taken. Everyone had to stay in position and all arms had to be stock-piled under the supervision of senior ranks. It gave me some satisfaction when I smashed my automatic on the corner of the building and many more of my mates did the same. Futile, perhaps, but under great physical and emotional strain the action was just taken. No movement was allowed that night excepting for the usual moving about for brewing tea or eating cold food from tins. We tried to raise a little morale by singing the favourite song at that time which was 'South of the Border' but I'm afraid we were all off key.

The following morning (16th Feb., 1942) I, along with three of my mates were detailed to go to an Army food Depot with a 15 cwt truck and see what we could get before the front line Japs got there. It was very dodgy indeed and we were constantly running into bands of Japs, who had already set up road-blocks all over the city. Strangely enough they allowed us through without much bickering and were in a very amiable frame of mind, owing to the great victory of the fall of Singapore. Alas, when we arrived at the Depot we found that this was under heavy guard by the obviously well-informed Jap army.

On this journey we saw some terrible acts of violence, by the inebriated Japanese with the priority being to cut down as many Chinese as they could. There were bodies lying everywhere, many of them being decapitated and they hadn't even drawn the line when it came to children. It was humiliating to us to witness such acts and not being in any position to protect the poor wretches. We were allowed to make our way back to rejoin our unit, but not before one or two confrontations with the road-block guards. When we eventually reported back to our Bn. H.Q. everybody was collecting what belongings they had and preparing to face the 12 mile trek to the Changi area. I spoke of my being humiliated before but this was really something, when Regular Army units like the Manchesters, Loyals, Gordons, Argyles etc. had to trudge this long 12 miles of shame and frustration.

I think if any of our Officers had ventured a word of command at that time there would have been a lynching by the road side. To make matters worse for me was to be informed that my younger brother, Bill, was missing in action. It was ten days before he was finally rounded up, having been in action in the Bukit Timah area with the 2nd, 26th Bn. Australian Army.

It was very hard to accept the fact that the great fortress of Singapore had fallen to a 'load of Rickshaw pullers' and slant eyed coolies. How wrong we were and how we had underestimated these little yellow devils. After a few days celebration in Singapore and a grand victory parade the race continued through the Pacific islands sweeping all before them with the momentum of unstoppable confidence. My Battalion as Regular troops still thought that in a few weeks the Allies would smash back into the Far East theatre of war and gobble up these impertinent upstarts. Tokyo would be destroyed and Tojo would be strung up by the testicles for daring to come into our back yard. From this time there were just two types of human beings - optimists or pessimists. The optimistic managed to struggle through the next $3^1/2$ years and saw victory around every bend of the river. The pessimistic never made it.

Changi Realisation

Settling down in the Changi Barracks complex was not an easy adjustment. My Bn. was allocated what had once been the R.E. Barracks and bedding down was just on the concrete floor with a bit of manoeuvring to get a place on the open verandah. The buildings were two storey high and were also bug ridden. The Barracks had been unoccupied for many weeks and these bugs were ready to attach anything within reach. A psychiatrist would have had a field day here when the numbness of defeat finally abated and the realisation that we could be here for years started to sink in. Most just accepted the situation but there were some who just sat down, refused to eat or speak and just died. I had heard of low mentality natives with the power of just willing themselves to die but never thought of seeing it in my own race. One of my own platoon was the first to go in this fashion, a man who was a rough tough old campaigner but maybe a bit short on the tenacity or will to survive. On the second day of our incarceration the Japs arrived at the entrance to the Barrack Block, dropped off a few sacks of rice, some vegetables and three or four massive open boilers or 'qualleys'. The first day after this 'drop off' was to be spent building up a kind of Field Kitchen, which would fit the qualleys and I really think this job in itself raised an interest to be up and doing.

I was detailed to the 'heavy gang' whose job it was to forage for timber for the kitchen fires. We had one or two giant axes and Heaven knows how one of our Officers managed to 'procure', borrow, or nick a cross cut saw. Armed with these we proceeded to a wooded part of our area and soon had a considerable load of wood, which had to be loaded on the chassis of an old Army 15 cwt and hauled back to Barracks.

The rice and veg. diet was not exactly conducive to heavy physical exertion but it was amazing how the fat of our earlier good living was trimmed off and replaced by muscles we never thought existed. One of our younger officers (who was a member of a nationally known Whiskey firm) had a 20 stones weight problem but a month attached to our 'heavy gang' soon took care of that.

For a month or so the Japs left us to our own devices and we had access to a swimming 'pagir' on R.E. Point, but this privilege was soon taken away when some of the boys gave with the 'Harvey Smith' to one or two small Jap Naval craft, which were limping in after some action or other. From that time we were securely wired into our own allocated area and any unauthorised straying from these areas would be classified as a 'break-out' which could have meant shooting on the spot.

Each unit was issued with a Jap flag and we could visit our wounded in Roberts Barracks, provided we proceeded as a disciplined party, headed by a responsible person, carrying the flag. This privilege was known as the 'Flag Ferry Service'. The route to 'Roberts' was the main road, and strategically placed about every 200 yds were armed Sikhs, who had defected to the Japs. They were part of a formation known as the Indian Free Army, who had 'Volunteered' to join the East Asia Co-Prosperity Sphere and would fight on the Burma front if called on. This rabble was headed by a fanatic known as Dillon Singh, who was reputed to be an Anglo Indian with a hatred for the whites. Although these traitors strutted around and took a delight in making each Flat Ferry party do a proper march past with the customary 'eyes right' or 'left' whichever side of the road they happened to be. There is no doubt that the Japs also despised these people, and on one occasion I was one of a party proceeding along the road in an orderly fashion, when one of these bearded wonders started with the bullying tactics of making us repeat time and again the march past procedure. Whilst this was going on a Jap Staff car pulled up and the Officer sat watching for some time before jumping out of the car and approaching the big 6ft Sikh. He made him stand to attention and then took away his rifle/bayonet. Coming over to our party he brought out the biggest and strongest man, a chap known to us as the bully of the prison camps - Teddy Trapp. Teddy was a typical Scouser and always aware of his great strength, even his many tattoos had muscles. Anyhow, the Jap Senior Officer led Teddy over to this Sikh and invited him to take a swing at our tormentor! Teddy was naturally very wary and suspected the worst when the little Jap pulled out his whacking great Samurai sword, and we all watched with bated breath. After more prompting and threatening gestures with the sword Teddy gave a half hearted slap to the face of the Sikh and then awaited to catch his own head if the sword came into play. The officer showed extreme annoyance at the obvious 'pansy slap' from such a big chap as Teddy and indicated that the next blow had to be delivered with more enthusiasm. Now the Sikh was standing to attention with his back close to a rubber tree and when Teddy delivered the next one backed up by all the pent up hatred in his big frame, the crack could be heard from a great distance. The Sikh's jaw had definitely shattered and I'm not sure that the tree wasn't splintered as well! The Jap sheathed his sword as the big sentry hit the deck and then proceeded back to our party making a big show of feeling the biceps of Teddy, who was looking extremely flushed with success, satisfaction, or even both. The little Jap chauffeur was ordered to bring some 'Bull' cigarettes from the car and with many enthusiastic cries of "Presento" "Presento"! the fags were handed all round with an extra packet for Teddy. Such was the erratic behaviour of our captors which was to be seen on many occasions during the following three and a half years of captivity - sadistic one minute - benefactors the next.

Borehole Gen.

Life dragged on from this time, with now and again a calculated rumour that the Yanks were coming or the British had broken through on the Burma front etc. etc. The source of these rumours were referred to as No. 1 borehole or No. 2, the boreholes being 10ft holes which had been bored into the ground with huge manually manipulated boring tools. This was operated on the four man round and round action and some comic or other would be sure to make us 'roll in the aisle' by mooing like an ox. What were the boreholes for? Well, we erected a box like structure over these holes and hi presto! A toilet, also the thrones of the great thinkers who would forecast the war's end within a matter of weeks or if feeling pessimistic maybe a matter of months! The fantasies dreamt up by these lads was amazing and just because we wanted to believe we got a tremendous lift. The 'Trickcyclists' would have had a field day here.

Occasionally work parties were picked up and taken down to the Docks area, of Singapore Harbour, to off-load or load supplies on 'Troopers' then making their way to Sumatra, Java or known these days as Indonesia. It was the accepted principle to pinch anything by way of medical supplies, foodstuff, clothing etc. and many were the escapades on these dockside areas.

Nippon See All

One time I was one of a party detailed to carry cases of food up the gangway and onto one of these utility vessels. The Jap in charge was known as 'Jimmy Cagney', owing to his mannerisms and general air of cockiness. He spoke quite a bit of English (or American) and was a great source of amusement to us. One day in particular he had caught one of my party nicking a small tin of fish so decided to give us a lecture on the immorality of this act, because as he pointed out, stealing was unknown in his country, and only the thieving Europeans stooped to this, all that is, excepting their gallant allies, the Germans! Whilst delivering this lecture he had placed the small can in position just to his rear and every now and then he demonstrated by putting his hands to his face in binocular fashion and quoting "Nippon see all", "All men pinchee, pinchee but Nippon soldier see all". Just then a party of thieving Aussies passed to his rear and one of these lads must have fancied some fish for his dinner because the disappearance of the can coincided with their passing. When 'Jimmy Cagney' turned round to retrieve the can he couldn't believe his eyes and wasn't very amused, when one of our lads reminded him that "Nippon see all", sometimes but not always! It appears that the Diggers were "thieving bastards" as well as the Poms! If 'Jimmy' had found the culprit I think he would have presented Digger with his chips to go with the fish. Another time one man was caught pinching some soap and was made to eat some of it. He developed a sprinting prowess up to Olympic standard when the soap eventually settled in his stomach. At this time the Jap guards were front line troops and on the whole weren't too bad once you sorted out the star system of rank, i.e. no star - recruit, 1 star, 2 star and 3 star in seniority. The 'no-stars' were fair game and the general 'dogs-bodies' and 'kick-abouts'. We could frighten them without much effort.

Black Hole Of Selerang

We were just settling down to accepting little food, enough to keep us going, when the Imperial Japanese Army put the clog in by issuing a printed form written in English stating: 'I promise on my honour as a soldier, not to attempt to escape whilst a prisoner of war with the Imperial Japanese Army' .... Signed. This was totally against all the principles of the Geneva Convention and also against all our teaching as a member of the Armed Forces. The forms had their uses on the forementioned 'boreholes'. The Japs issued an ultimatum that all forms would be signed and handed in by the end of the third day or serious consequences would follow, but this was one time when our heels really dug in, no matter what.

On the third day our Officers were taken away and we were informed that they would face a firing squad. We still didn't budge and the order was then issued through senior N.C.O.'s that we were to form up on the road outside the perimeter fence and make our way to Selerang Barracks, formerly the home of the Gordon Highlanders. We loaded everything we possibly could by way of medical and cooking utensils etc. on to our 15 cwt chassis and set off the couple of miles carrying our personal effects on our backs. These barracks had been built for the installation of one Bn. of Infantry, at that time about 1,000 men and all equipment, but here was a situation where the Japs were going to cram in 17,000 men, who had to find cooking space, toilet space, sleeping accommodation etc. etc. We were like sardines but the flat topped roofs eased the situation. The only water supply was via standpipes, about six in all, situated at various points around the barrack square. The Medical and Cooking staff were supermen and managed to sustain us during the four days we were in this position. My own C.O. (Col. E.B. Holmes or 'Eb') was the senior soldier these days and was the only Officer with us during this dreadful period.

The inevitable had to happen when typhoid broke out and also diphtheria which could have been a killer. However, we still opted to stand fast until the threat was made to drag all the wounded and sick in from 'Roberts Barracks'. Col. Holmes had no alternative but to give in and verbally ordered us to sign the new forms then being issued, but to bear in mind that this was being signed under duress and on his orders, for which he would bear full responsibility. In other words, if the opportunity presented itself, go ahead and do it.

I would like to point out that escape was practically impossible,(1) being white in a brown community and the large reward offered by the Jap authorities for the return of the heads of would-be escapees, (2) and the most effective, the 2,000 miles of jungle to traverse into Allied occupied territory.

When I saw the great 'Colditz Story' and compared their lot with ours I could have sworn. They were either in Sandhurst College or Butlins Holiday Camp. At this time we still had the remnants of our K.D. and even had boots but when they were finished we were to get no more, but I digress.

McArthur Interlude

Back to Changi area and the dispersal of various parties to various places of work. My brother and I always managed to be on the same working parties. Our first job was the dismantling of the old Ford Motor Works on the Bukit Timah Road and being billeted in an old Army camp of timber structures being known as McArthur Camp. We had to bury a few stinking decomposed bodies and scatter lime all over the place but all in all it was quite comfortable and dry. 'Tansy' Lee soon had the rice boilers in position. By this time I had a six months growth of whiskers and 'Tansy' always bowed low to me and called me 'Saint Thomas' before threatening to "batter me with the Cross and drown me in the Font". He was a confirmed atheist and showed it, but to me he was a great friend as well as being a very cheerful extrovert.

I best remember 'Tansy' in the days just before the Far East war broke out, when we were being forcibly advised not to withdraw our monthly credit accounts but to subscribe as much as possible to the 'Buy a Bomber' Fund. We considered we were being paid little enough as it was, in comparison to the industrial workers and went ahead with our written applications for our credit accounts because a pint in the hand was worth two in the Company Ledgers. We had to parade,at the Company H.Q. and back our application up with verbal request, explaining why we had to have these extra coppers. What a carry on! At that time I was on 5/3 per day, and for that my body belonged to my country. Most of the requests were turned down until it came to 'Tansy's' turn and when his plea was believed he promptly fainted! The C.S.M. was screaming his head off - something about "dragging this so and so body out" and the young subaltern was just bleating like a baa-lamb! I dashed for a bucket of water hanging on the 'Fire Buckets' rack and promptly sloshed it over 'Tansy' on the deck. 'Butch' Lomas had also decided on the same action but didn't notice that the bucket contained sand until it was too late, so there we had 'Tansy' well and truly sand-blasted. Fred Karno never saw anything like this in all his military career.

Back to McArthur Camp and the dismantling of the heavy plant items in the Ford Motor Works. Incidentally this was the venue of the signing of the cease-fire or unconditional surrender and the Board Room in which it took place was still kept intact and sealed up.

Our job was to strip down and crane load all the intricate machine parts for despatch to Japan. Most of us had no knowledge of this type of work and what didn't come apart with a spanner was given the treatment with big hammers and chisels. It was just so much scrap when we had finished and overloaded on the overhead crane slings, much to the chagrin of a 'townie' of mine who drove this thing. The overloading caused the fuses to shoot out round his ears like meteors and he wasn't very pleased when one managed to get down behind his collar. The Officer in charge of this job was a Capt. in their equivalent of our R.E.'s, who had to wear a leather type mask owing to much of his features being missing. In spite of the fearsome image he presented, he wasn't such a bad character and was even known to 'presento' a few fags now and then when he was particularly pleased with any aspect of the job. I must say he must have been very easily pleased, and I can only assume that empty spaces where there was once machinery indicated to him that we were doing our stuff. He obviously hadn't seen the 'big hammer' operations wielded by we demolition experts. The final week on this job was more or less a yasme*, with a bit of cleaning up here and there, and on the last day we were loaded on to Jap Army trucks to be driven back to McArthur Camp and from there back to Changi and boredom. The forementioned masked officer, known simply as 'The Mask' saluted us as we left the Motor Works, possibly because he was delighted to see the back of us.

Goodbye Changi

We had hardly got settled in at Changi when the 'borehole rumours' started again. 'We were all being shipped to some Swiss Red Cross Camps in the northern Malay territories.' There would even be running water and this to us would be the very pinnacle of luxury. My dream at that time was to have a hot bath followed by a pint of ice cold beer and

* Yasme - holiday or rest.

then to sit down to a paper bag full of fish and chips! Dreams dreams, all dreams.

Came the day when about 200 of my unit were detailed to get everything packed for the following morning as we were going on a long journey to these supposedly Red Cross Camps. If we had only known! The roll call on the day of departure was chaotic with the Japs insisting on us numbering off in Japanese ichi! nee! san! see! go! etc. etc. We just didn't want to know, so it evolved into a pushing, jostling exercise, pretty much like a sheep-dog trial. At last we started off in Army lorries, all standing and holding on to each other on the bends.

We suspected the drivers were trying to get rid of their human cargo en route. On arriving at the Railway Station we again went through the sheep dog trial thing, only this time being split up into parties of 37 and bundled into closed-in box wagons. There was no room to sit or lie and when the sliding doors were closed the heat was oppressive to the point of suffocation. We eventually got under way with many screams of "Buggerah" and "Kurras" from the Jap guards. Just before pulling out of the station the guards undid the locking pins on the sliding doors and put the catchment on the slide runways, so that the opening was just about two feet. Even with this opening the people at the extreme sides were in a suffocating position, so that we had to take turns at the opening to keep us going with air. Everyone accepted the situation and I never saw one attempt at cheating, but I shudder to think what the outcome would have been in the event of any panic! This nightmare journey had to go on for three days and nights, with many stops onto shunting sidings to allow priority troop trains right of way travelling south. We had one meal of 'rice only' per day together with a pint of water, which had to be conserved where possible to spread out over the 24 hours.

One memorable occasion I managed to brew some tea with water from an outlet tap on the engine boilers. It tasted like nectar and was also an addition to our normal ration also proving to me that 'stolen fruits taste sweeter'.

Although we knew we were heading north all the time we had little idea where we were going because any small railway signs had been blacked out. Eventually we pulled in to a siding with timber platform and complete with sign stating 'Bam Pongh'. This was it apparently because the screaming guards started up once again, no doubt trying to impress on some of the local population that they were the masters and the white coolies were trash:"Buggerah! Buggerah! all men off", with rifle butts flying indiscriminately and boots flying out in all directions. I heard one of my mates claiming a penalty for being fouled!These were the lads who helped us to retain our sanity and gave credence to Rudyard Kiplings: 'If you can keep your head...etc.

We were formed up in some semblance of order and marched through this little tatty looking village until we were led through some bamboo gates, past a guard house and formed up on an open piece of ground, which was the centre of some attap-roofed structures. The first thing we saw was two poor wretched Thais who were on their knees in front of the guard house and tied up with a bamboo pole pressed across the calves of their legs so that they couldn't move. A rope round the neck was also securely fastened to a bamboo pole and a sadistic Jap Officer was belabouring them with his sword scabbard. Although not knowing at the time that was our first view of the dreaded 'Kempie Tie', who were the Jap version of the Gestapo. Even the Japanese O/Rs looked terrified and made up for their discomfort by screaming abuse at us.

After a while we were allowed to fall out and find our own resting place on the split bamboo slats inside the attap buildings. These slats were about a foot above ground. There was a back wash of water, sewage etc. from a stream running close by. This filth was lapping just under the slats and the stench was awful. We were to endure this for three days during which time there was much 'bashy-bashy' for the slightest so-called offense, probably for just forgetting to bow to the guard or wandering sentry. Oh yes, we had to go through the motions of bowing even though you were grinding your teeth and muttering obscenities at the same time. The name of the game at all times was humiliate the white dogs. These days when I am asked if it is possible to forget and forgive I could spit!!

As I have said earlier we had our comics who kept our spirits up with one antic or another. One time I was one of a party having to go past the guard house and the chap in charge was one 'Shifty' Baum, who was of German extract and a Chief Petty Officer in the American Navy. He was quite a character and his descriptive language was to say the least flowery. 'Shifty' didn't have a crack with you but rather invited you to 'come down here, Chuck, and let's shoot shit'. Anyhow, on this occasion as I say, I was one of his party, and the "eyes right" or "eyes left" had to be shouted out by the party senior, in this case 'Shifty'. The Japanese for eyes right was 'Kasra Niggi' and for eyes left 'Kasra Naggi' but not to Shifty! His variation was 'Scratch your dickie' and 'Scratch your knackers' shouted out in the proper parade ground manner. The Japs were delighted at this great show of respect. Shifty was one of the crew of the Yankee Navy boat 'Houston' which was sent down with the fish just off Jakarta (Java). It was known to the Yanks as the 'gliding ghost of the Java Coast'. Always the spectacular! We half expected Errol Flynn dashing through the Camp gates at the head of the 5th Cavalry. We were thankful to leave this stinking place and once again being banded on to trucks for the short run to Kanchanburi. This was a clean place and the attap roofed buildings were fairly new, commanding a view of the coming together of two great rivers The Mekong and the Kwai. The river was in full spate at the time and we were held up for a couple of days before the 'pom-pom' boats would attempt the crossing. The method was to link up sausage fashion anything up to six barges and hitched on to the 'pom-pom' which was really a small tug boat. We were grossly overloaded on to the barges and the tug pushed off facing the fast flowing two river link up. It was a trial of strength between the flooded rivers and the poor old 'pom-pom' and the instant the current caught the barges they swung round, the end one in which I was a passenger was arcing round at an alarming rate until brought to a check on the end of the chain. The tug pilot must have been very expert to control this little lot. We proceeded across in a crab-like fashion until eventually hitting the opposite bank all of ¼ mile further down stream, where we smartly tied up to the friendly trees. The tug pilot had to make a further two trips in this fashion and I considered him to be a very brave man indeed, even though he was forced to do this against his better judgement. Our column then set off upstream and after a walk of about two hours came to this huge camp complex - Chungkai.

Chungkai Starto

This was to be the Base Camp for all the operations on the notorious Death Railway which was to claim 19,000 lives including around 500-600 of my own unit.

It was now January 1943 and we were to be white coolies for the next two years, constructing a railway from Chungkai to Moulmein. Chungkai being linked up by this time with Bam Pongh and thence to Bangkok in the South.

The attap buildings were quite good at that time. The split bamboo shelving on which we slept was about three feet up off the ground. The apex roofs overlapped on the outside and the sides were completely open which meant we were practically in the open except for the attap roof, and our allotted space was one metre each. Talk about Hitler and his Lieberstraum!?

The first day on the railway was a con trick. When we arrived on the cleared area we were confronted with bamboo profiles and a piece of string linking them up to the required height. It was then explained to us by an English speaking Jap that we would be split up into parties of 20 and each party would have the measured out task of filling in and conforming to the strings. On completion of the task we could all 'go yasme' until the following day, but emphasis was put on that the task must be completed before we were allowed back to camp, even if the big dark came. We thought we were on a good thing when the task was completed by midday and fair enough, they allowed us back to Camp. The ground in this area was peaty, easily dug out with our 'chunkels' and loaded on to stretchers with long bamboo poles pushed through for handles. God knows what we would have done without bamboo, although later on these same sharp spiked plants were to be the cause of hundreds of amputations starting with a small scratch, and then going through the cycle of ulcers, rotting flesh and then into the tissue and bone. (Again I digress as these conditions weren't experienced at that time.)

The second day's task was a much bigger job and the allocation of work was added to daily so that we were practically running to complete before returning to camp and rest. This gradual work load must have been compiled by a sadistic mathematical genius because the guards became more and more aggressive as the weary P.O.W.'s strove to get the work done.

Mutiny

The officer in charge of this section of the railway at that time was one Kerihama, a baby faced monster who had our Korean guards shaking at the knees. Hence the pass on of plenty of bashing, face slapping and kicks, indicative of hysteria. This period was to be the first show of determined mutiny on the Railway. It started over a trivial flash of temper when one of our Sgts (Bill Whitehead) showed dissent to a stupid order from the Korean sentry, known to us as 'Nutty Nutty' owing to his liking for a nougat like delicacy sold by the local Thais. Bill was immediately ordered to stand on the top of the embankment, holding a heavy rock at arm's length above his head. Now Bill had been badly wounded in the knee and strain of this nature was excruciating but nevertheless he stood for quite some time in the blazing sun with the sweat dripping from him. The British officer with us at the time was Major Buchan of my own Regt. - a gentleman in every sense of the word and the courage of a lion. Our work force were known as 7th Battalion, comprising of the Manchesters, Gordons, Loyals, Argyles and a few 'Swede-bashers' or Cambridge Bn. All were regular Army units and, as professionals we were expected to set the pace or the mood. The sight of this young Sgt. set up in this undignified position by this stupid Korean was too much and first one man threw down his chunkel, pick or 'tongah' and others followed suit. We indicated to the guard that either Bill was relieved of this punishment or we just sat down. The guard started shouting for reinforcements from other work unit sentries, who immediately fixed bayonets and closed around us. We had no intention of giving ground and it looked very 'dicey' until Major Buchan ordered Bill Whitehead to step down from the embankment, just as Kerihama arrived on the scene. The Jap was enraged to the extent of threatening Major Buchan with his sword and ordering him to take the place of Sgt. Whitehead. The Major just turned his back on this gibbering monkey and gave out the order to down tools and fall-in in orderly fashion, to ignore the threatening sentries and prepare to march back to Camp. The thought flashed through my mind that this order would go down in Military History under the heading of 'Famous Last Words'! To live, to die, who cares, was the general feeling and I think Kerihama realised this because he backed down with a lot of 'egg on his face'. We marched off in parade ground manner as only Regulars can do, picking up momentum on the way and joining up with other work parties en route until we reached camp, to be immediately confined to our huts under menacing pointing machine guns. The stage was set for a massacre when the tension was broken by the Jap Camp Commandant advancing on to the Officer's Quarters and taking Major Buchan with him, presumably for a Court of Enquiry. The atmosphere in the whole camp was charged with menace and we were ready for anything, even to having a go with pointed bamboo poles, which had been collected for just such an eventuality. After about two hours of discussion between the Japs and our senior officers it was decreed by the Camp Commandant, that the rest of the day would be a 'yasme' and all would be forgiven. There was to be no further action taken, our rights of 'honourable soldiers' to be recognised, and there would be no 'bashing' except in extreme cases of insubordination, which was the code in their own Army. Although we weren't happy about the last part of the statement we had to accept, and all in all we considered we had a victory which tended to give us some uplift of pride. About this time the Yanks were sending 'Lockheed Lightning' twin fuselage Recce planes over the Bangkok area which provoked a nervous re-action from our captors. One day we formed up for a lecture on security and an officer known as 'Winkie-Pop' was told to pass on the gist of the so-called security rules to the prisoners. This officer had a nervous twitch and to all appearances was winking one eye whilst talking. The Jap instructions was delivered in this vein - "Come-look-round-go-back-speak-plane is Joto Nei (no good). Go-back-come-back bump! bump! ala men die. Fire in big dark Joto Nei! O.K.?". Poor old 'Winkie' relayed these instructions to us with his customary nervous winking. The Jap accused him of double dealing by telling us of these restrictions at the same time neutralising the order by winking!! From here on the officer was taken away to the Jap guard house and rumours ran rife, some stupid, some comical. One of our lads made up the most outrageous story that Winkie was wheeled in front of the Jap Commandant, who threatened to shoot him on the spot whereupon Winkie begged him not to do this but to shoot five men of the Manchester Regt. instead! We all knew this was a 'make up' but was typical of the times and brought a little light relief. Another time one of the Korean sentries managed to fall down one of the crude slit trench toilets which were all of 8 ft deep. These trenches were the home of millions of crawling maggots, and boyo landed smack in the middle of them with loud hysterical screams which could be heard at Bangkok. It was nearly dark at the time and one of our lads offered his hand to pull him out, but there was an ulterior motive, because just when it looked like a clear 'lift up' for the sentry he was promptly dropped again. This happened three or four times with the Korean getting more and more hysterical. The sound of his screams brought some of his mates running, whereupon his British 'helper' shot back to his hut, having considered he had done his 'bit' for the day. This Korean was one to avoid for quite some time from then on! No gratitude at all!

Then there was the lunatic Jap 'Gunzo' (Sgt) who was in charge of the 'Pom-pom' which called twice a week with the rubbishy vegetables and rice which had been allocated to the Camp. He could be heard half a mile before the boat rounded a bend in the river, shouting his head off for the offloading party to be ready. Sometimes he even took out the sword and swung it around his head like a one man landing party on enemy territory. He was a proper 'nut case'. One day whilst in the middle of all this jumping up and down, flashing sword etc. - he fell into the river!! The water was about 10ft deep at this point and he couldn't swim. Again some of our lads, who were there at the time, offered him 'help' but nearly succeeded in drowning him by thumping him on the top of the head when it appeared above the water! The Thai boatman had to spoil it by fishing him out with an old car tyre. Boyo was very subdued on the next few trips until his confidence returned, but from then on he was treated more of a joke than a menace. By this time we were starting to get organised and part of the camp had been allocated for a 'hospital', staffed by one or two of our own overworked Medical Officers.

The first sign of overwork, malnutrition and exposure was now apparent. This, coupled with Malaria, Dysentery, Beri Beri etc. made skeletons out of once healthy young men. The amazing thing here was the fact that the older men appeared to have more stamina to withstand the constant ravages of overwork and underfeeding. Also the fact that the bigger you were the harder you fell, or so it appeared. What was really happening was the set ration of one pint of rice per man, per day, could possibly sustain the smaller man, but the big lads were really on starvation rations and were also expected to do more work because of their greater strength. This way they were being clobbered left, right and centre. Added to this was the cock-eyed philosophy which at that time was 'no work, no eat'. Quite naturally our belief was entirely opposite and every effort being made to give the 'byoki' (sick) people more without cutting down too much on our own meagre rations. Although there were the odd bad apples in the barrel, the vast majority accepted that the sick were in greater need than the 'not so sick'. What it really boiled down to was that rations were cut down all round, causing all the relevant ills associated with lack of physical strength to combat. Dysentery, Malaria, Pellagra and Beri Beri were all part of every day life, and until such time as they brought on complete collapse of the physical frame, were not even considered as being an excuse for not slaving on the notorious railway. The modern expression of 'flogging a dead horse' was applicable in this situation, and one would have thought that better feeding would have speeded up the work. The I.J.A. (Imperial Japanese Army) were determined to complete this project, the ultimate aim being to pour reinforcement and supplies into Burma and consolidate their gains. About this Mountbatten, Wingate, and Bill Slim had other ideas and once the tide had been turned at Imphal the going got harder for the I.J.A., so much so that the railway slaves were on the receiving end of more and more 'bashi, bashi' consistent with the 'speedo' principles of our yellow masters. We jokingly referred to ourselves as 'Railway Maggots' as against the big business 'Railway Magnates'. We now moved into the big finance era when the Japs decided to pay us the princely sum of 10 cents per day (officers 40 cents). This windfall could purchase on the 'black market' two bananas, or two eggs (duck). A saving of five days pay could buy a packet of 'Red Bull' cigarettes or a hank of crude oily like native tobacco, which had to be rolled in dropped tree leaves, toilet paper (if any) or the best of all - bible or prayer book pages! There was more than one reason for calling it the 'good book' and what could be a religious comfort to some was much more a comfort to the less holy of us.

Looking at the suffering all round puts an awful strain on the religious beliefs which had been implanted in us from childhood but some there were who formed little groups of prayer debates, but alas their many efforts to convert the vaster majority of the unholy, met with derision. One self appointed apostle in my own unit was Tug Wilson, who could be heard quoting passages from the bible at the drop of a hat. To me, Tug was a keeper of days in that the only indication of time was his weekly Sabbathical rendering of 'The Old Rugged Cross'. How he managed to keep count was a complete mystery to me as one day just followed another, starting with sunrise and terminating with sunset - being helped along with taksan* manipulation of the bamboo rod; the rifle butt or the boot. I got what I considered to be more than my share of this treatment being a natural rebel with a temper to match. It was common to be floored three or four times in any one day, but the trick was to get up to attention again before the boots came into action. To be beckoned by one of the guards with the curious upside down gestures of the fingers meant only one thing, and one had to brace up and prepare to be stood to attention whilst the Lord and Master attempted the delivery of a K.O. More often than not the blow would land high up on the head and sometimes hurt the attacker more than the attacked, in which case the Jap would get more and more hysterical, eventually resorting to the use of the rifle butt. Even though the body would be wracked with pain it was a blessed relief to be ordered back on the task and seek anonymity amongst the slave herd.

During the early days in Chunghai the officers had maintained their own class distinction by taking over two of the long attap roofed buildings and prepared to sit or lie out the rest of the war, not all, mind you, but some! The only shake up they had was the officer in charge duties on railway work parties or tenko** parades. The Medical Officers were the only exception to this state of affairs and they really gave of their best with so little to help them.

Officers I can remember in this field, who gave outstanding service were Markovitch, Kevin Fagan, Dunlop etc. Dr Markovitch was the amputation expert, and many of the later called Amput Battalion owed their lives to this black bearded straight talking strong man. The scratch from the poisonous bamboo spike would start off as a mere pin-prick which would develop into huge stinking ulcers two or three inches across and eating down to the very bone. The primary treatment for these horrific festers was to scrape out with a sterilised spoon all the decayed flesh and maggots which had been deposited by the thousands of 'blue-bottle' flies. No anaesthetics, no nothing, just a cold blooded scrape out job, whilst the sufferer was held by an orderly or a couple of his mates. The wound was then covered with leaves from the trees, if possible banana leaves because they covered a larger area. The ulcer hole had first been filled in with the magic blue powder which was guaranteed to send waves of pain through every fibre of the body, and usually gave peace to the patient by rendering him unconscious. When the ulcer still insisted on spreading the decision was then made by Dr

---

* Taksan - plenty/much/lot of ** Tenko - roll call

Markovitch that the limb had to be removed to save further suffering. This so-tough man's attitude changed when gently informing the patient of his decision. In the event of heavy blood loss there was usually a stand-by donor from someone of the same blood group. The blood group details were on the fibre medallion which had been issued to all serving ranks, previous to the outbreak of the Far East War. Some had been lost but I was one lucky (or unlucky) enough to still have mine round my neck like a dog collar, and as a consequence was on the list of volunteers. I still have a little piece of paper which states - 'I see that you have given blood for your comrades. An act which, under the present circumstances as a P.O.W. is highly commendable.' - Signed Col. Outram. Chungkai, 1943. The patient named on the paper is Sapper Evans, so some boyo could still be around through the efforts of Dr Markovitch and myself. The blood was pumped in direct and I should imagine had a 50/50 chance of success. I never saw this chap again and can only hope that the 50 was on the right side of the oblique stroke.

About this time a mad Irishman was admitted to the Camp with a story hardly credible but eventually accepted by the majority. It seems that Paddy was in a party of R.A.F. personnel, who were despatched to Australia, when most of the antiquated aircraft on the Singapore base had been destroyed. The intention was to make use of these skilled men in the R.A.F. but after arriving in Australia the project was dropped so it was back to Blighty for the lucky dogs; Singapore having 'fallen' by this time. Paddy had formed an association with a 'Sheila' during his stay and knowing Paddy it could have been three or four. Anyhow, on the day of departure from Australia Paddy had overslept, having granted himself an overnight pass ashore. He arrived at the quayside to see his boat sailing into the golden sunrise and no amount of blarney could turn it back. There were all sorts of enquiries flying about by the time Paddy had convinced the benevolent Aussie authorities that he was an ex-wounded hero from the raging inferno of Singapore and wasn't always sure of his whereabouts. He was in clover, and was allowed to return to his Sheila to await shipment on a later boat. Alas for Paddy, this old cargo boat just got as far as the Sumatra Seas before being torpedoed by the now all powerful Nipponese Navy. As to whether he was lucky to be picked up by the enemy is all a question of how you looked at it because I do believe that Paddy later died on the 'Railway'. When he arrived at Chungkai he was fitter than most and promptly set the wheels in motion to gain outside contacts for the supply of 'Sam Seu' (Whiskey), Quinine, atabrin etc. in that order, the one being the luxury and the other classified as a dire necessity, and that again was a matter of how you looked at it.

During the course of events I was persuaded to join the team of smugglers purely for the hell of it and I suppose I would get a kick out of putting one over on the Japs. The expeditions were organised to coincide with the so very rare yasumi* days. The time and physical effort was out of the question on a normal work-day. Any drugs procured in this fashion were handed over to the Medics in the camp and by way of a bonus the Sam Seu was sold to the wealthy officers.

On our second trip we set off as usual through a secret gap in the bamboo perimeter fence, first having evaded the patrolling sentries and even through the sparsely vegetated jungle into the open ground beyond. The whole journey was only about two miles, but took quite some time owing to our security system of sending forward one of the party as scout and awaiting his return before proceeding. Our goal was a few native huts out in the wilds, there to be admitted by a pre-arranged whistle signal which admitted us into the presence of four villainous looking Thais armed with parangs. There were usually four in our party, each carrying four water bottles ready for filling with the potent brew for which Paddy handed over a roll of Thai dollars. After a short stay and a couple of goodwill drinks with the Thai gentlemen we were on our way back heavily laden with the brew and any medical supplies the suppliers could let us have. There was much less caution on our way back, the couple of snorters dulling the fear instincts and giving us a devil-may-care attitude to the whole thing. This was to prove our undoing on this particular trip when negotiating the run-in through the fence. I was bringing up the rear of the party of four when pandemonium broke out with screams of 'Kurrah! Kurrah!' The first two of the party managed to break through and escape to the darkened billets but my companion and myself finished up pinned to the fencing with rifle at throat. The swashbuckling attitude had left us by this time and the only thing that appeared to buckle were the extremely shaky knees. A bayonet touching the throat isn't exactly conducive to brave thoughts of conquering the world. After a few rifle butt smacks and leg kicking we

* Yasumi - rest

93

were unceremoniously pushed down in the general direction of the guard house, still carrying our illicit cargo. One of the sentries gave his verbal report in a high pitched tone and one would have thought they had captured two generals on the field of battle instead of the two half starved wretched un-armed P.O.W.'s. We were made to off load our water bottles and then kicked into the 'sweat box'. I must tell you about these sweat boxes! They were made of the usual tightly woven bamboo slats and were similar in design to the one-horse trailer boxes, dimensions being about five feet in length, three feet wide and four feet six inches high. These cunning dimensions ensured that one couldn't stretch out in any direction. Any demands of nature had to be done 'in situ' and there was already evidence of previous occupants - in situ! What with the bashing, the stench and the thoughts of impending punishment we weren't exactly singing 'Bless 'em all'. Strangely enough, the guards were singing the Japanese version of this song and it dawned on me that they were swigging the evidence and having a high old time. Poor Alec Guinness must have had a very harrowing time in that sweat box on the Kwai Bridge Camp, where he spent seven days. We had just one night in this hell-hole before being released early next morning, first of all getting the usual kick-about from the still inebriated guards. Whether they had drank all the incriminating evidence or wanted to retain the remainder was a matter for conjecture but the fact remains that we scarpered back to our huts covered in bruises but happy to have escaped so lightly.

There was one bright spot for me in this Camp and it came about this way. A N.A.A.F.I. like structure had been set up by the officers, who were allowed to make bulk purchases from the native traders and retail to the boys. They had a cookhouse (or squeeziebar) to the rear of the structure in which they cooked their purchases of tapioca, sweet potatoes, pork, peanuts, sometimes even scraggy looking chicken. This one bright day was my birthday and I was feeling at rock bottom when my Brother wandered in to our hut with an old piece of towel draped over a mess-tin full of a delicious food purchased from the N.A.A.F.I. He had flogged his only precious possession (a 'fob' watch) to get me this birthday dish and I don't mind saying that I broke down and wept, only to be told by Bill to "shut up and eat up". So much for brotherly love.

Christmas 1943 brought out a rash of the 'speedo' periods and the termination of work on this particular section of the 'Railway' when orders were then issued for our work battalion (7th) to prepare to move up the jungle to our next sector. The great trek began by the skeleton like army of barefoot coolies and woe betide any who fell by the wayside.

By now all our original possessions were worn out and the typical kit comprised of one Jap Happy or loin cloth, one hat (of a sort), maybe half a blanket, a half mess time with a bamboo spoon and again bamboo in the shape of a cup unless you were lucky enough to have retained an old tin of some sort. No footwear excepting for a pair of slip on 'clip clops' made from old pieces of wood, with a top strap of old cloth or leather from an old 'ammo' boot. Thank God for the odd comedian who could even make humour out of this situation by singing a bit from a movie: "We shall dance up the Avenue". Dysentery and malaria were cutting down our numbers and the trek was a nightmare of requests for "speedo benjo's" (quick No. 2) until the guards got fed up of such requests and the rifle butts came into play at every excuse. Many of us were suffering from the inelegantly phrased 'Changi Balls', which was the result of lack of vitamins, bringing on such an internal itch in the scrotum that men were known to tear at themselves to such an extent that the testicles came through the scrotum itself. The other obvious result of the vitamin deficiency showed itself in semiblindness and 'happy feet', the latter being agonisingly painful and depriving the sufferer of sleep even though half dead through fatigue. We slithered and slid along the muddy banks of the Kwai helping each other along, carrying the meagre belongings of others until the first Camp hove in sight - 'Wun Lung'. We thought we were home and dried but this was to be a brief respite only for a meal of the normal pint of cooked rice and some watery stew, which, we were told by another comic, was garnished with scrapings off the cook's clogs. Nevertheless we were thankful for food in any shape, form or substance. This was the only meal we were to receive in any one day's march because the Japs were sticking to the golden rule of 'no work no eat'. An hour's 'yasumi' and then trudge on to the next camp, reaching there at night fall.

Wan Tekkin Camp

Wan Tekkin was to be our home for the next two months. Things weren't too bad here because it was the food distribution centre for all the Camps to the North. This meant a bit more food for the camp inmates and allowed us time to recover from previous deficiencies. Efforts were still being made to help the very sick, one of which was the selling of 'coffee' lashed with an ample quantity of 'gula malacca' which was a brown sticky raw sugar substance. The 'coffee' was 'synthetic' in that it was simply raw rice, burnt to a black state over an open fire and then ground down with a piece of male bamboo. It resembled charcoal and come to think probably tasted like charcoal if it weren't for the 'gula malacca'. This brew was made over an open fire, the water being drawn direct from the Kwai which helped to give colour to the concoction. The selling was strictly controlled by the senior officer in charge and we took it in turns to hank the 5 gln tins around the camp to the old street cry of "Hot sweet coffee", or "Hot, sweet and milky" - subsequently changing to "Hot, sweet and filthy". The price charged was 1 cent a 'pialo' or pint and in the darkened huts tasted more like coffee than coffee. The proceeds were handed over to the officer who used the money to buy extra eggs or fruit for the very sick.

Against the express wishes of all P.O.W.'s Far East, the Emperor of Japan had a birthday whilst we were resident in this camp and the Camp Commandant decided to give us a yasumi day by way of celebration. Extra rations were to be issued including one tin of pineapple chunks and the ultimate in meat rations of one live bull buffalo. This animal was large, I can tell you, and the very thought of pole-axing the beast was going to present some problems to the chap who professed to being a slaughterer by trade. The buffalo had a rope sling fastened round the neck and was gently led to a large tree in the compound, the rope then being twined round the base of the trunk with four men on the end of the rope in tug-o-war fashion. The slaughterer was only a small chap but was armed with an axe-like weapon, blade one side, iron spike the other and known as a pole-axe. This huge creature submitted to all this treatment without an aggressive move even to having a mud centre mark on the forehead just below the horns, and this colossus had horns! The butcher took careful aim before bringing the spike down on the mark with all the strength at his command. The buffalo dropped to its knees, appeared to roll over but suddenly came to life again with terrific roars. The four men hung grimly on to the rope while the executioner took careful aim again for another swing of the pole-axe but I think the roars of the animal must have un-nerved him because the next effort had no effect, not helped also by the fact that two of the men on the rope had fled the scene along with most of the spectators. The buffalo stood with head lowered, the blood running down the face whilst the remaining two rope men stood their ground. By now, the slaughterer had admitted defeat and looked helplessly about him when up stepped the bully of the prison camps - Teddy Trapp, complete with tattoos, the swagger of the city guy and by now armed with the pole-axe, which he had taken out of the nerveless hands of the butcher, who promptly left the vicinity. By now, most of the spectators; were sitting on the lower branches of the surrounding trees and watching with fascination as Teddy took careful aim with the weapon. The very first swing made three things happen at the same time: (1) the axe handle broke, (2) the bull went berserk and (3) Teddy and the two rope men broke all records to the nearest trees with the bull in staggering pursuit. They just managed to clamber to safety as the animal lurched beneath them heading for parts unknown. To safeguard the rest of the camp the armed Jap guards had to go on a hunt to try and despatch our meat on the hoof. We were told afterwards that the three prisoners taken with them were handed the loaded rifles to finish off the wounded animal whilst the Japs took cover. The carcass was quickly cut up and taken down to the boiling pots in time for an evening meal, and what a meal! The Japs had abandoned all security and got down to some serious 'saki' drinking whilst we pleased ourselves what we did.

One would have thought that the Japs would realise the sense in better feeding for better work results, because there is no doubt that everything evolved around the fairly good supply of rations and the associated low sick numbers. Nothing of any note happened in this camp excepting the occasional bashing and even these were less than the norm.

Oh! there was one crop-up from the previous year and that was the magical appearance for a short time of 'Jimmy Cagney' of "Nippon see all" fame. We suspect that he was an English speaking plant by the Jap authorities, who were increasingly nervous about the infiltration of genuine news passed along the grapevine by a chap who owned most of the river 'pom-poms', although we weren't to know this until the war's end. Although some of us recognised 'Jimmy' he didn't appear to recognise the now near-naked lads, who were part of his work party on the Singapore Docks, and strangely enough, where he spoke quite good

English in those days he now professed ignorance of our language! We maybe all looked alike to him and a good job too, because we had the opportunity to pass the word to "keep ears open and gob shut".

All too soon the section of railway allocated to this camp was completed and we were soon on the move again, this time on a three day 20 kilo a day trek. It was now noticeable that we had less and less to carry owing to the bartering which continued all the time with the thieving natives, although, in all fairness our own people were conditioned to this way of life through sheer necessity and knock for knock was an accepted principle.

The travelling was lighter but still the rough terrain had to be negotiated and months of heavy work with little food had taken its toll. By this time I was around 8st. - quite a drop from the original 11st. of hardened bone and muscle of the Battalion football, rugby, and hockey teams. Weightwatchers take note! The trudging along with the occasional kick from the guards was spent in fantasy, when the mind wandered away from the body. First I would be on the Fell Road looking for birds nests, then 'dooking' in the beck which came straight out of Ennerdale Lake, wandering down past Hazel Holme, Wath Bridge, Cleator Mill and then onwards down the valley to eventually flow into the sea at Sellafield. I was then a boy again rolling 'paice eggs' down the Lonney, maybe waiting the return of racing pigeons to my Father's loft. Happy was the man who could adjust his mind to this condition because it was the safety barrier between sanity and the depressive drop into hell. This latter state was the start of the 'give in' stage and the will to live deserted the mind. Many bodies were either burnt or maybe just left to rot on these in-between marches, depending on the mood of the morons, who drove us until we dropped. They prided themselves on being able to maintain a certain standard of fitness whilst the 'joto-nei' (no good) prisoners allowed themselves to get Malaria, Dysentery, Beri Beri, Vitaminosis, Pellagra etc. etc. Considering they were clothed and netted against the onslaught of the malaria carrying mosquitoes, were well fed, did no work, had supplies of all the necessary drugs and had good covering against the monsoon storms, it would have been surprising if they had been in our state.

Bahn Kow Camp

Our next camp was Bahn Kow and the first thing to greet us when we finally stumbled in was the sound of a big drum beat, emerging from a timber structure which was raised up off the ground. There were a few native huts to the rear of this building and the P.O.W. camp was 50 yds short of this complex. There were three 'qualleys' or boilers set up ready for boiling up our rice which had been delivered by river boat previously, also a certain amount of timber blocks ready for firing under the boilers. Whilst the cooks started on this task the remainder just claimed their own lying down space on the split bamboo shelves in the attap roofed buildings, before being allowed down to the fast flowing Kwai, which by now was in spate owing to the tropical monsoon weather. Nevertheless it was heaven to just hang on to the long 'lallang' (grass) and allow the down rushing brown water to envelope the body, although this rushing stirring up of the sandy bottom gave problems to people who had been advised to have circumcision. It may be a bit of a giggle now but very distressing at the time. I'll never forget squatting in a circle with many more sufferers and dangling the swollen organ in boiled up water in a tin can. On looking round the circle and noting the various expressions I exploded into uncontrollable laughter and this in itself was worth all the man made medicine ever pharmacised by the pharmacists!

The stretch of railway task allocated to this camp would be about 5 miles and fairly flat terrain, but was nevertheless arduous in that the daily walk to and from the camp was an ordeal in itself, especially now that we were experiencing a very hot dry period, the temperature soaring away over the 100's. The naked bodies were practically black, and the dried sweat left a lime like covering of salt which attracted 'humble' bees and other insects. It also caused a permanent raging thirst, which, if not appeased could render a man delirious and eventually bring on an unconscious state. Various camps are associated with a happening at that particular time and usually of an unpleasant nature. The first distressing situation forcibly brought home to us, how far we had deteriorated from the accepted code of civilised behaviour. On this particular day the heat was oppressive and the 'speedo' was being applied by the bullying Korean guards. We were a long way from the river which meant two of the work-party had to strike off at a tangent from the work area to try and reach the only source of water. Two hours later, when we were practically dead on our feet, these two characters could be seen approaching, bamboo support poles on shoulder and the two water 'fantazzies' swinging between them. There was a rush to form a queue, drinking tins at the ready, and awaiting ½ pint per man, this being the usual allocation and even this quantity would just be a stave off for a very short time to our dehydrated bodies. All hell broke loose when it was realised that the water containers didn't contain any water at all! This was the only time I witnessed the guards protect prisoners from their own kind! These two wretched men had to stand behind a ring of four Koreans armed with rifle and bayonets whilst two or three prisoners were trying to get to them with shovels. It was frightening to witness such animal behaviour. The Jap Engineer in charge had no option but to call off the job for the day and allow us to return to camp in a half-crazed condition. All the necessary ingredients were there for trouble with a big 'T', and only the low physical condition of the prisoners prevented a blow-up, that, and the pacifying influence of one or two officers who appeared not to want any trouble at practically any price.

Our old Chungkai friend, Keriama, was in charge at this time, aided and abetted by one 'Charlie Chaplin', two sadists together; one a Shoko (officer) and the other a Gunzo (sgt.). One day Keriama decided to have a booze-up with friend Charlie and then vent their exuberance on an officer of the Gordons, who had shown dissent during the morning of that day. The officer was tied had and foot in a kneeling position in front of the guard house until such time as these two louts had drank their fill of Saki and sang a few soul-stirring victory songs. Charlie had a pet monkey on a chain which received more kicks than pats but this was to be its last day of torment before being despatched with one swing of Keriama's sword. I really thought he expected applause from the silent crowd of prisoners who witnessed this act, instead of which the look of disgust drove him into a hysterical rage. The two then advanced on to the guard house where the Gordon Officer was tied up like a trussed chicken, but one of our officers, Major Buchan, was already on his way to plead for mercy for the young officer, who by now had given up all hope of seeing the next sunrise. These two mad-men were in no mood to listen to any pleas but rather decided that two trussed up prisoners would be more fun and lend an element of competition to their sword play. It was ordered that Major Buchan be similarly tied up and lined up alongside his brother officer in full view of the prisoners, who by now, had prepared a variety of heavy or pointed objects in case things got too far. The preliminaries to an execution then began with the two drunks advancing in a step to step fashion, brandishing the heavy two handed swords over their heads, and going through the motion of taking aim on the forward bended necks of the two victims. Every step nearer produced a scream-like shout to try and terrify the two. The officers had never flinched during this ordeal and we were very proud for them. This sword play continued for quite some time whilst the fully alerted guards covered us with rifle and bayonet, but one could see that they were really terrified of the consequences if the two Japs carried out their obvious threat of decapitating the luckless two. This was the most explosive situation since the Chungkai mutiny and on the face of it boded no good for Major Buchan, who was the central figure on that occasion. I know one thing for sure if the Japs had carried out their threat, they, along with the guard would have died an unpleasant death. The determination of the P.O.W.'s could be sensed at this time and no amount of rifle fire or sword swinging would be any deterrent. Keriama and Charlie must have sensed the build up of hate and disgust, so much so, that they ceased their activities and ordered the two officers to be unbound and sent back to their quarters. The two were drained of all feeling and zombie like in every move but still walking tall. We considered this a victory and strangely enough we were never again to be baited by either of these two. Keriama was eventually hung in Changi Jail on the termination of the war for his brutal handling of P.O.W.'s on the Burma Siam Railway.

The Regulars

Many months of hardships had welded together a mixed community of various splinter groups from 'The Manchesters', 'Loyals', 'Argyles', 'Gordons', 'Leicesters' and 'Surreys', all regular serving troops. The workforce was to be known as the 7th Battalion and where in normal peace time conditions, prior to the war, there was intense rivalry on the sports fields, boxing rings etc. which sometimes spilled over into the many Bars in Singapore, here we were all brothers and 'muckers'.

As an anti-climax to the 'speedo', kicks, slaps and general knock about administered by the Korean guards, there came a day when, on returning to camp we were confronted with a large screen structure set up in the village clearing. 'All men' were invited to attend a cinema performance put on by the generous Japanese authorities. The only snag was that we had to sit behind the screen whilst the Jap guards and Officers (who had been brought in from adjacent camps) sat to the front. To say it was hilarious is an understatement! It was all propaganda material showing the Japanese forces over-running the Phillipines and Java, being welcomed by the 'grateful' natives, who were thankful at being liberated from the white imperial devils. All salutes were left-handed because of our behind the scenes position, and on one occasion, when the Emperor Hirihoto was shown, the Jap community leapt to their feet with screams of "Kirrah! Kirrah!". They had hardly squatted down on the ground when he was shown again on the screen and this same procedure had to be carried out five or six times during the cinema show. Far from being a relaxing hour it developed into a P.T. parade!

Before leaving this camp we were introduced to the primitive method of bridge building, there being two dried up stream beds, cutting through our camp section of railway. A pile driver was fashioned out of a section of teak tree, and spikes or 'dogs' driven into the top to which was fastened ten ropes on either side, these to be fanned out symmetrically, the outside ropes being the longer. The ropes were then looped through a metal hoop which was the apex of a wig wam formed triangle of trimmed down trees. These days this structure would be known as a 'dead man' in the steel structural trade. A shallow trench was dug into the rock hard ground to encase each of the two previously shaped foundation trees into which had been cut holes strategically placed to hold the 30' trimmed upright poles, which were to be the mainstay of the structure. The 'dead man' was set in position over each upright in turn, with the ropes looped through the iron ring fanned out on each side and manned by 'one man, one rope'. The engineer in charge then sat on a seat of a sorts which was part of the 'dead man' and chanted the time for rope pulling to bring up the pile driver and release in unison, on to the top of the upright. The chant sounded like "eno-ni-ma-syo-ma-syo!" over and over again until the monotony sent the rope pullers into a stupor of ox-like similarity. The chanter was always referred to as 'the monkey on a stick', and many were the attempts made to dislodge him off his perch by trying to get a bit of top spin on the ropes by an uneven drop. Alas, we were never successful and so the chant went on "eno-ni-na-syo-na-syo!" Ten or twelve hours on this activity interspersed by short yasumis could really put you on your 'chips'. The trudge back to camp, perhaps two miles, was an ordeal in itself when the body was drained of all 'fight-back'. During these daily returns to camp I kept trying to remember a poem from my school days - 'The Church bell tolls the knell of parting day' - but I could never get past the second line before numbness took over the exhausted mind. Maybe tomorrow I'll remember, unless God (if there is such a being) will take me out of my misery. This job was to last for some weeks with "taksan shikota - squashie mishie - yasumi nei" (plenty work - little food no rest). Even though we knew that all roads lead to the 'Three Pagoda Pass' on the Burma-Siam border, we weren't too unduly bothered about the next move. Keriama was left behind on this occasion and the new Commandant was the 'Nazi' who proved to be a very strict disciplinarian but just and although he had his own special brand of behaviour could be very amusing with his Hitler mimicry. Apparently he had been on a military mission to Nazi Germany and was very proud of the swastika on his tunic. The biggest crime you could commit in his Camp was in not saluting any member of the Jap staff. He didn't bother so much about the bowing part when not wearing a hat so long as you gave a 'bara salaam' (big salute). Came the day when we left Bahn Kow and headed north with 'The Nazi', heading the party as if we were going for a two mile walk.

On The Move

We were three days on this march but 'the Nazi' had to fade out after half a day after demonstrating that 'all men' would continue the march at the same pace as he himself had already set! He was a prize clown, all right! The evening of the second day was a hair raising experience, which wasn't so apparent at the time but viewed in the cold light of the following day was frightening. Just before dusk of that evening we were given the order to rest but not to take this as being the 'big yasumi'. After about an hour we were then 'coaxed' to our feet by the ill-tempered guards and made to flounder on in the dark over very rough terrain indeed, which assumed the proportions of a climb more than a walk. Small lights could be seen twinkling in the dark en route and guide ropes were set up in some places. Each light was held by an unknown body in the dark, who kept calling out warnings like 'Watch your step!' 'Steady as you go' etc. etc. After scrambling along this rough track for some hour or so we started descending towards the sound of the river, still unaware of the few yards to each side of the route. We were to know at first light next day, because this was the location of the notorious Wan Po bridge and we had actually been scrambling across a cliff face with a 200' drop to one side! Faced with this obstacle in the cold light of day I don't think many would have attempted it, but as it was I don't think we had one casualty excepting cuts and bruises on the bare feet. Another half day's slog brought us on to a part of the river which had done practically a 'U' turn and was to be known as Monkey Bend.

Monkey Bend

The Camp was a motley gathering of old tents through which could be seen the stars at night or in the event of a downpour became a shower bath. Our side of the river was a backwash of shale and gravel beds and the river looked cleaner here than at any other camp location, due, no doubt, to the gravel beds which acted as filters. The opposite side was very thick jungle and occupied by a large school of baboons who never ceased night and day giving voice in a howling crescendo of sound. They no doubt resented our presence and made it unsafe for any body of less than 20 men to go down to the river. Malaria was bringing men down at a high rate, and 'all men' were made to take 6 quinine tablets per day so as to maintain fitness for the job in hand. This overgulping of quinine brought on deafness and many a man received a rifle butt for disregarding orders from the sentries. As well as the deafness the resultant condition was to having a floating sensation and stupid, sluggish reactions, often referred to as 'drug drunk'. To counteract this the 'Tijo' (The Nazi) hit on the brilliant idea of having P.T. classes. *Before* proceeding to the railway! The prisoners were sectioned off into classes of 20 men in each and one team pitted against another in competition, the grand prize for the overall winning team being a large sack of peanuts. It is hard to imagine that any man of normal intelligence could believe that the robot motions of 20 tottering wrecks would create men who went around kicking sand in people's faces. I think it was a form of subtle sadism designed not just to humiliate but to break the spirits of the hated British, who never tried to hide the fact that they were superior in all things. When the occasion was right the Jap or Korean guards were told that "Churchill No. 1, Tojo No. 10". This opinion didn't amuse them at all, but rather brought on a rash of 'bashi-bashi' and 'Taksan shikota'. The stay in this camp was of comparative short duration and preparation for the next move began with the terse statement that "all railway finish next camp, plenty speedo before monsoon". If we had been in hell up to this point we were soon to be cast into the fiery furnace from now on, and starting with a long trudge for 6 days, when only the build up of hate kept us going and the determination to see those animals get their come uppance. Many fell by the wayside due to the ravages of malaria, dysentery, or just out and out starvation. We weren't even allowed time to bury the dead and, in fact, the drop outs were subjected to bestial behaviour from the guards until no amount of kicking could raise them from the coma which preceded blessed death. All sense of time had gone by this time and it was just a matter of daylight - come dark - come daylight etc. We passed through some camps which had been re-claimed by the jungle but all had the sickly sweet smell of death with here and there an arm or leg protruding from the putrid ground, having been brought to the surface by the now lashing monsoon rains.

Throughout the whole of this time Tug Wilson was insisting that there was a God and we were all God's children - even the Japs. Looking around it wouldn't appear so, but this tall gaunt man was adamant even though he had the wild gleaming eye of the unbalanced, but hadn't we all? After what seemed a life time of staggering along, slipping, falling and helping each other we eventually came to a bamboo palisade, which had been previously built by the 'clearing' party whose job it was to remove trees and bush from the line of the proposed railway and clear areas for camps to be set up. God knows how many of these lads died. The only signs of cover against the monsoon rains were a lot of old tents lying here and there, already sodden and well tramped on into the foot deep mud. A series of rice boilers had already been installed on the bank overlooking the river and a month's ration of limed rice stocked up under the old attap roofed structure. This rice was a canary coloured concoction and along with the husks of newly cut rice, was supposed to cure us all of the ills associated with lack of vitamins. It was vile, and full of maggots but at our low ebb of starvation the lot was forced down - even the maggots. We considered the maggots to be our meat ration!

The few officers in our party were called to the Jap guard house and instructed that we would be required to start on the new section of the railway on the following day, but a special 'bridge party' had to be detailed comprising of 30 fit men because the work was extra hard. I don't think there was 30 fit men in the whole of Thailand, but nevertheless I was to be one of the unlucky gang. There was now incessant rain for 24 hours a day and our old sleeping tent which held 15 men was dripping all the time saturating the inmates. After a meal of pap-rice and small quantity of sugar we were marched out to be introduced to our 'virgin' section, the bridge men having to walk on a further 2 miles or so to a depression running across the line of the track. This was to be the start of about 5 or 6 weeks under the 'gentle' care of the worst sadist on the whole of the railway.

The Mad Gunzo

The 'Mad Gunzo' was ably aided and abetted by the 'Monkey' who just thrived on lashing out with anything he could pick up. The 'Gunzo' was an R.E. Sgt and was a real genius in the art of bridge building with just bare materials from the surrounding jungle, some dynamite and a lot of 'dog' spikes. Trees to be used on the bridge erection were blaze marked and two men with axes detailed to drop them before shooting them down the steep incline to the site of the operations. With four or five pairs doing this work at different levels it proved to be extremely dangerous (a) from the falling trees and (b) from the stripped logs shooting down the incline. The very first day one man had a broken leg and had to drag himself back to camp, the alternative being to sit in the rain and await our return to camp in the evening when we could have rigged up a carrier stretcher. He opted for the 'lone ranger' effort - anything to get away from the two maniacs in charge, but as it was, we had to scoop him up on the way home after dragging himself for 3 or more hours. This chap was delirious, and, in fact, didn't survive the ordeal but died a couple of days later.

There was a lot of rock to be blasted on this location and about 20 men were coupled off for hammer and jumper work driving the ½ metre holes into the solid rock, one man sitting legs astride and holding the jumper whilst his mate swung the 10lbs hammer. The 'jumper' had to be eased and twisted after every clout with the hammer. When the 10 holes had been driven to their required depth the charges were inserted, but it so happened that owing to the uneven density of the rock strata some holes were ready before the others. There was no waiting. The mad 'Gunzo' would touch the short fuse with his cigarette end before making a dash for cover, whilst the unsuspecting workers were toiling just a few yards away. The resultant injuries gave him great pleasure apparently, but injured or not the job had to proceed as normal with no recognised break for the 'mid-day' rice which had to be eaten whilst standing in the rain. This maniac even demonstrated a quick method of scooping the rice up into the mouth in a shovel-like manner, whilst his small sweat towel was draped over his 'mischi' tin to keep out the torrential rain. He appeared to have some difficulty with his cooked 'stink' fish. We didn't. We didn't have any!

An incident happened here which nearly cost me my life. I was driving in some 'spike' dogs, into the partially completed section which would be about 30' high. I had my back to the straight drop and smacking away at the 'dogs' with the heavy hammer when it slipped through my hands. A combination of imbalance helped by an 'aerobatic' Kung Fu kick from the mad Gunzo sent me completely over the edge and only the overhang bamboo scaffolding saved me from being maimed or even killed. As it was my outstretched arm quite accidentally managed to wrap round the bamboo pole and swung me like a pendulum before dropping me into the raging torrent beneath. I managed to scramble out some 20 yds further down the ravine, but the chest muscles on my left side were badly torn and made all movement agonising. I was to suffer this agony for many months, and where complete rest for the injury was the only cure, here it was unthinkable.

The Legion Of The Damned: Cholera

Thousands of Indian Tamils, Malays etc. were now being drafted into the area to speed up the work on the railway. Our own hygienic arrangements were very crude, but were non-existent to these coolies. Subsequently the death rate from dysentery etc. was atrocious. Just at this time the real killer struck - Cholera! I watched men die and practically dehydrate in 24 hours. All body fluids just drained away, and the victim died from the feet up, starting with agonising cramp. After 24 hours or less the body was unrecognisable, being of skeleton proportion. Of the 15 men in my old tent 10 were to succumb to this dreadful scourge and we would 'sick' joke with remarks like "See you in Hell". I considered we were already in hell so had nothing to fear.

The bodies had to be burned right away and there was a constant coming and going to a jungle clearing where a pit about 4' deep x 10' square had been dug. We arranged the bodies like kindling wood with a layer of bamboo between each row of bodies but this was not very successful owing to the heavy rains and there being no fat on the bodies to facilitate a quick burn. The funeral pyre was lit once every day but on taking more bodies the following day, the half burnt carcasses of the day previous would have adopted grotesque positions of sitting up and sometimes leaning on each other. We had to try and push them down with long poles so as to get the next load of bamboo in place. Carrying out this duty one day and having no footwear I managed to slip on the side of the pit, finishing up between two half burnt bodies. The hair stood up on the nape of my neck and was to remain that way for many days. The very disturbing factor was the absolute lack of feeling towards the dead, even the close friends of yesterday became something of a nuisance when just a dead body to be disposed of. The dead would be lined up on the ground, sometimes covered or half covered in straw sacks and placed on rice sack stretchers or 'tongahs' ready for picking up by the burning party, first there automatically picking up the lightest looking body. That we could be brought down to this sub-human behaviour would have been unthinkable a few months before.

The Jap guards and other staff were living outside our camp area, also our senior officer (British). This didn't exactly endear him to the luckless P.O.W.'s and from then on he never had the ordinary courtesy of recognition, whereas on the other hand we had two Medical Officers working amongst us, who fought for us all along the line. Sterling chaps who saved many lives and risked their own, working among the Cholera victims.

I had a weird experience during this period when I either had a dream or a visitation. A good friend of mine had been one of a few transferred up the line to the 211 Kilo Camp, the mission being to clear the area for the next camp site. Unfortunately the cholera epidemic had spread up and down the area and news filtered back of the many deaths sustained by this party. This night in particular I had a vivid dream that Tommy (friend) was talking to me and asked if I would take his personal belongings back to his sister in Salford. It was so real that I practically touched him and then woke up in a lather of sweat, even though the night was wet and cold. Up to this time I wasn't to know that Tommy had indeed been a cholera victim but I was to receive proof a few days later when one of the party from 211 back in Tarkanun asked for me by name. On finding me he handed over a little waterproof bag which held a Catholic prayer book attached to which was a metallic cross. He said he had taken it from Tommy's body, and having heard him mention my name, had decided to hand them to me. Two years later I was to send these items to Tommy's brother for handing over to the sister. Dream? visitation? you tell me. He was a great chap, all round athlete, middle-weight champ, footballer etc. but this horrible plague brought down the strong as well as the weak.

Where we burnt our dead to the best of our ability, the thousands of native coolies just left their dead where they dropped, so that in time the place stank to high heaven and no doubt prolonged the epidemic.

The Japs decided to sort out the 'carriers' and to this end they would take rectum slides using a type of chop stick for this job. A mate of mine had ulcerated feet and couldn't walk to the roll call and line up for the 'bum-stab' so I volunteered to carry him, both being covered by an old ground sheet. The Jap 'horse-doctor' came down the line with an orderly in attendance, who was popping the 'chop-sticks' into glass phials held in a box. However when it came to my friend's turn I leant forward with him on my back but didn't expect the crude up the rectum, so much so that I jumped forward and landed both of us in the mud! The follow-on kick on the same part of the anatomy didn't exactly do wonders for my dignity, but a mental mark-up of hopeful retaliation some future date helped to pacify me. By this time the mind had been conditioned to acceptance of anything the Japs would, and did hand out, but the memory storage of each kick, slap or butt was the only thing that kept most of us alive. I never once doubted that I would eventually get home and the episode of the 'Visitation' helped me along that line of thought. If there was a life hereafter my friend had indicated that I was a safe bet for returning his personal belongings. The only worry in this direction was the continued decline in health of my younger brother, but I vowed to do all I could to help him through. I had a unique method of rousing him to want to take a swing at me. When I noticed a lethargic drop-away in his behaviour or movements I would try and pick a fight with him and the resultant re-action was like a re-charging of his batteries. What he *didn't* see was my emotional break down after each of these occasions. To witness this would have neutralised the whole object of 'operation shake-up'. The one thing that did spark some interest in him was being made an elephant 'boy', being the hooker-on of chain hooks to logs, the chains being harnessed to the elephant. This particular elephant was known as Chang, and Bill quickly became attached to it, being a great animal lover. He also threatened to punch the native handler when he resorted to punishing the beast by beating it on the forehead with a spiked club. The elephant had amazing intelligence and could scoop up giant logs on its two tusks and place them in any desired position on the bridge structure. It had moments of frustration when having difficulty moving some of the heavier tree logs or when the hitched up logs would slide forward on to its legs whilst going down a forward incline. He would throw his trunk in the air and squeal with rage, at the same time pounding his massive feet in a dancing motion. At such times his eyes appeared to change to red and I, for one, kept well clear, but Bill had complete trust in the unpredictable animal. When these situations arose the 'Mad Gunzo' would get all worked up into a rage on a par with Chang, and make the classical expression "Kurrah! Buggairo! Elephant no good! Come 10 men!". Moments like these we dreaded, because there was always a mad round of belabouring with shovels, bamboos, or anything which happened to be lying around. I think this Gunzo must have studied the noble art because he could plant a gloved fist right on the button every time. Granted this was made easier for him by the fact that the recipient had to be standing to attention, and so long as he could pick himself off the deck and stand to attention again he could expect another 'presento'. I held the record of 6 in a row for quite some time but was surpassed by the 8 times drop of our Bn. heavy-weight. I was perturbed by the uncertainty that I may be china-chinned. These semi K.O.'s were mentally referred to as being 'another one for the King' and no chance of the B.E.M. We were to construct two bridges under this mad genius before being pushed back on the quarry face job. Before we left him and his monkey faced henchman, what was left of us sang a song - "If I had my way, you would *never* grow old". We sang with feeling and he thought we were bemoaning the fact that we were going out of his area - the clown!

Takanun Quarry

The quarry face was a hard hammer and jumper job with added danger of a 100' drop to the jagged rocks below. It took a lot of concentration to hit the quivering jumper when first starting to break through the rock strata, but having done so, the metre long rod would be more rigid and being held in two hands by the other member between straddled legs, could be hit with more confidence. A lack of concentration on my part one day nearly had me over the cliff face, but as it was the shaft of the hammer came down on my right knee and paralysed all feeling in the leg. The knee came up like a balloon and meant I had to get back to camp.for some medical attention. Much to my amazement the guard allowed my partner to help me back to camp. It was agonising scrambling along the cliff face dragging one leg behind, terminating with a rope pull up to a higher level. My partner stood just below me whilst I pulled up on the rope and just when I dragged myself over the top shelf I found myself at the feet of a Korean guard, who made no attempt to help - not that I would have accepted it. As I dragged forward, the obvious injured knee presented a chance for this brute to give it a kick' The sudden shock nearly had me over the cliff face and, but for my Gordon Highlander friend, that would have been my lot. The red-headed Scot was quivering with rage and I thought for one moment he was going to have a go, but a maximum effort of self control ruled the day thereby saving his life. It took us two hours or more to travel the two miles back to Camp, Jock half carrying, half helping me in alternate hops. Up to that time I didn't have much liking for this Scot because I remembered him from the peacetime condition previous to the Far East War, when he was attached to the Red Caps and, as such, was one of the enemy to we rumbustious Regulars. The real jewels shone through when the going was hard and the little no account niggles of yesterday were as nothing in the present conditions.

The "come-look-round go-back - speak" planes were becoming more and more regular, and combined with the rush of Jap reinforcements making their way up through our area towards Burma, gave us a more optimistic outlook and around the end of 1944 we were beginning to see the light.

It was noted also that the reinforcements were but mere kids compared to the old China front campaigners, who had opposed us during the Malaya fiasco. These youngsters were dragging field guns through the mud, the overspill rocks from our quarry face, and over ravines. They were being unmercifully thrashed on to greater efforts by the few senior N.C.O.'s in charge, giving us mixed feelings of pity and exhilaration. The low standards of these reinforcements gave us the first inkling that the I.J.A. were scraping the very bottom of the barrel. The few days of my incapacitation gave me a chance of a desperately required rest but I was still worried about my brother who was in a bad way with malaria/dysentery, the one complaint always accompanied by the other, owing to the very low ebb of vitality through over work, starvation diet and exposure to the elements.

I was lying on the bamboo slats one day during this enforced rest period when I heard a voice singing - a real cultured baritone. The song was 'You are the harbinger of Springtime'! I listened entranced at the marvellous rendering and when the singing stopped I roused myself sufficiently to go find the owner of the voice. Nobody - just nobody! Did I hear it or was it just the quinine singing in my head? Whenever I hear this song my mind instantly flies back to Takanun, the Kwai and the jungle.

Whether the Japs in charge of the railway job were starting to worry about repercussions or reprisals I wouldn't know, but they decided to sort out the very sick from the people who just had malaria (not considered on the sick qualifications). We were lined up and inspected by the 'Horse Doctor', who indicated with the prod of a stick who would go back down the line as being of no further use to the mounting speedo period.

This was to be the grand-slam to complete the job and step up the influx of war materials and men, who at the moment were leap frogging from one completed section of rail to the next. It made us sick to the stomach knowing that the end result of our working and dying was to help pour reinforcements into the cauldron, which was now Burma. The outcome of the sick 'line-up' was that my brother was told to prepare for return to Chungkai but my 7 stone frame was adjudged to be capable of carrying on still further. The following day the sick were carried on stretchers or helped along to the rail pick up point but not for a safe journey in closed in conditions. The rail transport was the long flat wagons or open structure type entailing the lashing on with old belts, rope or tree bark strips. I fastened my brother on with an old belt and prayed for a safe journey down the 'switch-back' rails and round the cliff face pack of cards structures. Even though the journey was a hazard in itself I was glad to see him go from this rotten cholera infested area, where men were dying and being burnt by the dozen. It amazed the medical authorities, that during the whole of this horrific period, there was very few attempts at suicide. I knew of one case only when a man deliberately gashed his wrists on the pointed spikes of chopped down bamboo clumps. He regretted the action when the desperately overworked two doctors tried to save him but were too late. Other than this one isolated case most had the will to live and tried to fight off the ravage of Malaria, Dysentery, and even Cholera. Limbs had to be amputated owing to the eating into the flesh of jungle ulcers which sometimes reached the proportions of 3"/4" and boring straight down to the bone. Incredible though it may seem, men had to lie back whilst a spoon was used to dig out the rotten flesh and maggots. The smell of decaying flesh was sickening. I was lucky in that I never had this affliction but had everything going by way of Tropical disease, and as I told one medical orderly "I have so much malarial bugs in my system the mosquitoes won't come near me". To me the days and nights became as one until one night I found myself on the river bank, not knowing how I had got there. I just remember staring at the rushing water and trying to determine the reason for being there. Two days after I was to black out completely, but instinctively feeling just the icy cold then the fiery warmth. I was later told I had cerebral Malaria and was very lucky to pull through. After this close to killing bout I was never to be affected by Malaria again, so whether ! had built up an immunity I wouldn't know. During the next few days and at the non stop insistence of our two valiant doctors it was decided to sort out the more desperately sick and send down river to Chungkai. I was one of this party and so we were loaded onto river barges instead of going by rail.

Back To Chungkai

I don't know which was the more hair raising because the river was running fairly high and building up more en route owing to the 'feed-in' of minor tributaries. There were four barges linked onto the 'Pom-pom' and the system of stopping at the various camps down stream was to manoeuvre the 'pom-pom' to mid stream and then turn to meet the down flow. This action made the barges swing round in a dangerous manner, the tail end barge swinging round at an alarming speed before ending up with a bump on the river bank and after a series of bumps and near misses we eventually arrived in Chungkai.

After the terrible experience in the more remote camps up the jungle it was with a more optimistic sense of security that we struggled ashore to be met by many helpers, hot tea, and a meal of Nasi Goreng. We thought we were in heaven. My weight was down to about 7 stones and I had two enormous abscesses on the buttocks, added to this was the 6 months whiskers which made me unrecognisable to my friends. Efforts were made to clear up the numerous skin complaints and scabies by scrubbing hard until the skin was bleeding, then plastering on a sulphur paste mixed with 'Windfields' ointment. The latter paste was simply the anti-dimming ointment previously in use on the goggles of gas masks! The cure was infinitely more painful than the complaint but such was the feeling of self-disgust at the bodily conditions that we would go to any length to attain civilised cleanliness. My whiskers were shaved off with a sharpened clasp knife after a first trim with a pair of old scissors. During this operation (I use this word in the kindest sense) I was subjected to more cuts than the proverbial Chinese torture. It was even suggested by an onlooker that we catch the blood in a bucket and make black puddings. My protests at this Sweeney Todd's lack of finesse brought forth the information that he was employed for some time shaving and laying out the dead at Southern Cemetary Mortuary (Chorlton-cum-Hardy, Manchester). He couldn't remember any of these subjects bleeding, he said!

This camp was the huge Base for all the Camps to the north and as such, had better food and other amenities like a canteen, a concert party and even a football team! It was brought home to me in this camp how tough and resilient the human body can be and given half a chance, will kick back from any condition. Seeing my return to this camp no-one would have thought that I was to be taking a P.T. class of eager volunteers, who were desperate to get back to their former physique. I knew this was impossible but nevertheless there was a gradual improvement and more than that was the feeling of self respect and the pride that we had been through hell and now fighting back. After a half hour of physical jerks and gentle swinging exercises, there would be the jog down to the river for a swim and clean-up. I even played for 'England' in an International match against the Koreans, who had quite a good team! We were leading by six goals to none at half time but decided that it may cut down the many incidents of bashing if we allowed them to win by seven goals to six! Anyhow, bare feet against boots gave them a distinct advantage.

By now, my brother had a job in the 'squeeze-baa' (cookhouse) and was starting to come back to normal, but then the blow struck. The Japs issued an order that 100 men were required to go and construct a Hospital Camp near Bangkok. Once again I was one of the chosen and it looked like a separation from Bill until he heard of the intended move and was added to the party by R.S.M. Milne (Gordons). We took our last look at Chunghai before being entrained for the unknown destination.

Nakom Pathon

The day's journey was quite pleasant the weather being kind and we were on open trucks and travelling light. By now my worldly possessions consisted of half a blanket, half a mess tin, an old fruit tin for tea, a bamboo spoon, a loin cloth and a pair of home made Chinese 'cloppers' as footwear.

That was it, but as I say the advantage was travelling light and put us in the Bedouin category, and led one of my comrades to remark "the family hound has a better bed than I". The remark was made in a jocular fashion because nothing could have knocked that lad down, not even the fact that he was a pitiful wreck and the colour of an over-ripe orange.

The new hospital locality was on the outskirts of a town called Nakom Pathon and from what we saw of it it was one of the Buddhist holy places with a huge copper-domed place of worship. The sun would glint from the dome when at a certain angle.

The camp area had been agricultural land - about 1 mile square and the left over crops of tomatoes, mangos, sugar cane etc. provided good pickings for our half starved gang. There were two man-made ponds in the area and about six real timber buildings already erected by Thai craftsmen, as well as the usual attap roofed structures to which we were accustomed. We could hardly believe our eyes when we say the cookhouse all ready and stocked with rice and vegetables. After being lined up for the usual pep talk by the Jap Commander through the Korean interpreter (Four eyes), we were dispersed to our billets in the attap buildings and given the usual instructions. 'All men, yasumi, tomorrow taksan shikota' (today, rest, tomorrow - plenty work). Of all things I was detailed to work in the cookhouse! I had never cooked in my life but sticking to Army tradition that none of the cooks could cook I had to do my best (or worst) even though I could be guaranteed to burn the water. A remark often heard in normal peace time soldiering was "Who called the cook a ——?". Further to that - "Who called the —— a cook!?". 'Nuff sed. There wasn't much to make demands on culinary arts anyhow, just a matter of stoking the fires under the boilers, bash in the rice or the sometimes green stuff masquerading as vegetables, and alternately poke up the timber fires and the contents of the boilers, sometimes using the same paddle like implement. I did learn the trick of differentiating between 'Pap' rice (which required constant stirring whilst on the boil) and the dry individual grain cooked rice. The latter was boiled with very little stirring and then allowing the water to boil right off before withdrawing the fires and covering the rice with old sacks while still in the boilers. This could have been the forerunner of the 'pressure cooker' which allowed the contents to be steamed. We were three learner cooks on the same shift (again good Army organisation) and to our amazement nobody died from food poisoning. In fact, we were complimented on the standard of the 'lob-up'. We blotted our copy book one morning, however, when everything was going full steam around 5 a.m. and we decided to give an impromptu concert. We sloped arms with the stirring paddles and marched around the cookhouse area singing 'There'll always be an England', not realising that the atrocious singing could be heard from afar in the morning stillness. So engrossed were we in the singing and the jack-boot marching, (and you ain't seen nothing until you've seen this method in the bare feet), when we were virtually attacked by two outraged sentries who must have been having a 'kip down' somewhere. The usual 'che-atski'* was bellowed in our

---

* 'che-atski' - attention

ears and come to think, the gibbering shouts of the sentries could have been an improvement on the singing. Anyhow, we were lined up, disarmed of the lethal paddles and belted round the back with them. Previous to this we had carried out the fire embers and placed in a heap just out the front of the cooking area and to all intents and purposes the embers were dead. One of the sentries was to disprove this when, after giving us the going over he decided to stride through them in his rubber jungle shoes. He sank over the ankles in the red hot embers, some of which dropped into the half open tops of the shoes which he had probably loosened to ease the feet. Have you ever noticed how people who are so good at dishing it out are the world's worst on the receiving end? The gyrating actions of this character would have won all the 'rock and roll' competitions anywhere, anytime! His partner thought he had suddenly gone mad and dashed to try and subdue him, but that was his undoing, because he also took part in this rock and roll session. Then they both dashed back into the cookhouse, where there was two buckets of water. It was a dead heat and then the pushing and jostling began, each wanting to plunge the tortured feet into the water. We were aghast and awaited the revenge session from the two sentries but nothing happened so we assumed they were all burnt out.

Work went on apace at clearing the area of scrub trees, and it was here that I met a chap who lived near my own home village. After a month or so on the cook-house job I had been informed that I would never make a Cordon Bleu (I wouldn't know the ingredients anyway) and was being promoted to one of the 'heavy gangs'. To qualify for this you had to be about 9 stones but they must have thought I was a growing lad, and so to work digging out massive tree trunks, hitching on ropes and extracting from Mother Earth like a back tooth. Our gang were returning to quarters one day after completing our stint when we were ordered to help another party, who were having difficulties doing an extraction. I took hold of the rope next to a little chap, who was tugging, pulling and using a lot of Anglo Saxon expressions in the broadest Cumbrian dialect. After the successful outcome of this tug-o-war operation I asked him "What part of Cumberland, mate?", to which he replied "Egermuth - why?". I said, "I'm from the next village - Cleator". He studied me for a while and then said, "Well thoo doesn't sound like a Cumbria, but if thoo can understand this I'll believe tha. Ist ta gaan to hev yan afore thoo gaas". To which I replied "Aye, git em in"!

From that day John Proctor (sometimes called Harry), was to be right at my side through thick and thin. He was also to get me into numerous fights and arguments by falling out with all and sundry before informing his opponent that, "My mate'll tak care of thee marrer"! I was rapidly becoming punch drunk, until I informed one of his adversaries that I didn't know a Harry or John Proctor. He was a tough aggressive little character and afraid of nothing.

Rolling Out

When all the wood in the area had been used up for cookhouses, furnaces etc. it was decided to go further afield for supplies, and so about twenty of us were marched out this day under the care of two Korean guards. About a half mile from the camp we were confronted with a collection of old flat carts with massive wheels. We thought we had been promoted to the higher plane of ox, but no, the so-called ox were in a compound nearby and we were expected to harness these animals to the carts. The harness was a very primitive arrangement which consisted of a belly band with trailing ropes to fasten to hooks let into the front of the carts. The steering had to be contrived by a head-collar, and heaving ropes affixed to each side of the face of the poor animal, the idea being that the beast either turned in the desired direction or received a broken neck. The Calgary Rodeo was nothing compared to the action in this little compound. We were 'invited' by the guards to chose our own animal and 'saddle up'. Now these beasts had never been harnessed up before and being on the young side made no secret of the fact that they had no intention of being so. The big round up began and bodies were flying everywhere, helped by the flying hoofs of the indignant animals,until sheer exhaustion dictated that they gave in to be 'hoop-la'd' with the head collar and led towards the carts. The guards decided that one beast be harnessed at a time when 'all men' could gather round and practically lift the ox into position, before wrapping it up in all the trappings of the big heave ho. During this time the other animals were patiently waiting, being tied up to the rubber trees. This operation took nearly half the day because, even after harnessing, some of the cart shafts managed to get one side of a tree whilst the ox decided to go the other, to the great annoyance of the guards, who decided to help by belabouring the animals and the P.O.W.'s. We eventually got some semblance of order and the wagons proceeded to 'roll out' with we drivers or pilots standing on the flat carts to the many shouts of "Arrgh! Arrgh! Git along you mules!!" only they weren't mules - they were more stupid. Many were the mishaps en route when some of the beasts decided to eat grass or drink water by the wayside, one even managing to get into a paddy field before being 'persuaded' back onto the straight and narrow. On arriving at the desired location we saw before us huge quantities of wood logs, and these had to be loaded onto the flat carts and lashed on with spare ropes. After loading up the animals were faced in the direction of their home and given a few pokes to waken them up to the job in hand. Surprisingly they were more amenable to the indignity of pulling the heavily laden carts and I dare say the heavy loads steadied them down somewhat. The return trip took half the time even with the heavy loads; it was nearly dark when we reached camp to off-load the logs, which had cost much blood, sweat and tears (mostly with laughter). We were to make this trip about three times over the next few months and some of the lads started talking with a wild west brogue "Howdy, pard!" or addressing each other as 'wrangler'.

Medical Magic

The Chief M.O. in this camp was a Major Dunlop (an Aussie) and he was carrying out some marvellous operations with the crudest of instruments. He had such an air of authority that he was practically demanding various medical requirements through 'Four-eyes' the interpreter, or interrupter as one lad called him. One operation was a 'trepanning' job to relieve a patient of a brain tumour and don't ask me how he located the tumour without x-ray equipment? I had to give this lad a pint of my precious blood which I could ill afford, but still proud of the fact that the patient recovered and started seeing things the right way up. For quite some time everything was upside down and he was immobile. Patients were arriving from the jungle camps in ever increasing numbers and a great strain was thrown on the rations because the Jap authorities were still sticking to their ridiculous system of no work - half rations. This simply meant that everyone was on $3/4$ rations, hardly enough for convalescent prisoners to recover strength.

Volunteers for blood donors were required and a list made out numerically, i.e. 86 British 94 and so on. My small clan of

Manchesters/Gordons/ Argyles/Loyals/Cambs and Surreys were 100%, whilst not one of the Javanese Dutch put their name forward, although many of their own people required blood! This caused a lot of ill-feeling and we treated the Javanese like outcasts which, in fact, they were. They would dodge work for any excuse even though a heavier burden was being thrown on their compatriots. On one occasion on a sick parade line up the British M.O. decided to sort them out. The first patient had a thorn in his thumb, so the M.O. decided on major operation tactics by putting the knife or scalpel in the ball of the thumb, straight through the nail and out through the tip of the thumb! The rest of the Javanese drifted away smartly and very rarely bothered that M.O. again.

Now as any old Regular soldier would tell you, the game of 'Priest of the Parish' was an old Army pastime which involved punishments of a drastic nature being bestowed on the luckless slow-boys or non-abiders. The game would commence by all the participants sitting on the ground in a circle and each being christened with a name (some being of an Anglo Saxon origin). A leather belt or even a bamboo rod would be known as the 'Holy Dido' and be passed around for each member of the game to kiss it, thereby acknowledging its all importance. One of the participants had already been acclaimed as the High Priest and what he said was law - no matter what! The game would begin by the High Priest chanting "The Priest of the Parish has lost his considering cap, some say this, some say that - but I say Green Coat"! The player of this particular name had to be very quick by saying "I Sir? No not I sir!", "Who then, Sir", would be the reply from the High Priest - "Red Cap" and so on until someone would be caught on the hop. Punishment would then be meted out by the rest of the community and could be anything. I was caught out one night and had to go out of the hut, get on my knees in a worshipful manner and chant to the moon, "Allah be merciful, Allah be kind" etc. etc. I had to keep this up until called in by the assembly. Unfortunately, a wandering sentry came upon me and started walking round at a distance saying "Taksan Gelah" being a mixture of Japanese/Malay meaning 'Plenty mad'. He scratched his shaven head and must have decided that the problem was too much and had to be taken back to the Guard Commander. I really was praying that the assembly would call me in before his return, and to my ever lasting relief - they did. When I re-entered the hut there was two

The author, 1946

Jim Holden and Chuck Stewart, Wathgill Camp, 1935

Strensall Camp, York, 1935

Chuck and Holden

Surrender of Japanese General Yamashita, 'Tiger of Malaya'

Three Pagoda Pass, Thai-Burmese border

Japanese Memorial marking the point of entry to Singapore in 1942

Bedrock on the way to 'Hellfire Pass', 1994

Scotsmen sitting on the cross-members of the structure undergoing punishment by swinging their legs, finger in mouth and chanting an old Scots saying like this - "Uggle, shuggle o'er the Glen, I'm Daddy's Pet and Mammy's Hen"! - this being repeated over and over again. We were quite mad but the game had to be carried out in all seriousness. No-one outside the assembly had to approach or the order would be "Seize the unworthy outsider!". Whilst this "Uggle-Shuggle" business was going on the Jap sentry entered the near dark hut, and instantly the order range out "Seize the unworthy outsider!". We all moved together and 'NuttiNutti' (the sentry) flew for his life, dragging the rifle and bayonet behind him thinking we were all 'Gelah'. We decided to close down the game before an investigation was carried out.

Where before all rumours had been based on 'borehole' information now it was the 'Yellow Robes'. These people were students of some religious order, who were dressed in long flowing robes similar to an Arab burnous and all being shaven headed. They appeared to have the freedom to move around anywhere, being fed by the road-side traders and just sitting down whenever they felt so inclined. They were sometimes in small groups and some were known to have a smattering of English. The war situation was passed on by way of written notes and muttered conversation, the situation of opportunity being set up by way of a diversion which demanded the sentry's presence. The Yellow Robes could very easily have been Allied Agents, but in any case the news was always good and a boost to morale, in fact, I never knew any time in the whole of our time in captivity where optimism was on such a high plane, thanks in no small measure to our Yellow Robe friends; God bless them.

Alas another move was in the offing, some said back up the Railway, others said to Japan but the eventual destination was back to Singapore and a possible en-shipment to Japan. Before details were given to our few Officers there was a delivery of Red Cross provisions which, when sorted out, worked out at one parcel per ten men for cigarettes, boots etc. The food was all taken to the cook-house after the Japs had sorted out their requirements. I missed out on the boots but managed a pair of shorts and a vest. The Japs were not very enthusiastic about the cigarettes which had been given the not very diplomatic proprietary name 'Victory' cigarettes. How stupid could 'our people' be? We were already in hornet's nest without getting the backlash from a deliberate stir up. The fags were rubbish anyhow. This was to be the only Red Cross hand-out we were to get during the whole of our captivity, and worse than that was the fact that there was no mail, except a pre-printed card passed around which stated just the basics like 'I am alive and well' (alive - obviously, well - not so), "We are being treated well" etc. Because my brother and I were in the same camp at this time we hit on the idea of he filling in my details and me filling his. This ruse was to make our people realise that we were together. Assuming, that was, that the handwriting would be recognised. We had been P.O.W.'s for two years at that time so to our family we could have been dead, as many, in fact, were.

On the move again, passing through Bangkok and heading south through Ipoh and Kuala Lumpar, conscious at the time that we had now completed the full circle without disappearing up our own railway. On arriving at Singapore and being lined up for marching away it was so painfully apparent that this was not the Lion City that we once knew but rather a vast Concentration Camp, peopled by a cowed populace. The 'Greater S.E. Asia Co-Prosperity' was now being shown up as a sham, and rather than being a co-operative was in fact a fear ridden, starving community, ruled by a ruthless mob of power crazed robots. Not for them the clasped hand of brotherhood but the bludgeon of the victor, which was to lead to the non-cooperation and out and out antagonism. It was like giving a child a double-barrel shot gun and an invitation to go and play with the rabbits.

River Valley

Leaving the station in some semblance of military order but feeling humiliated in bare feet, Jap happy's or ragged shorts. The shocked looks on the faces of the few onlookers on our way through the streets was really an indication of the disgust they felt for the Jap overlords. Anyhow, after marching through this barrage of sympathy plus disgust we eventually arrived at River Valley Camp and there told to sort ourselves out amongst the dozen or so attap-roofed buildings. Once again I was detailed for cook-house duties which gave proof that my efforts in this line of duty at Nakom Pathon can't have been too bad. We were a real cosmopolitan crowd of P.O.W.'s by now - Dutch (white) Javanese, British, Australian and American. The only friction caused being the Dutch habit of 'dog-eating' when the chance arose, and when an Aussie had a puppy nicked and eaten there was a real International situation. The Aussie had pinched the puppy from the dock-side area in the first place, but he was prepared to share his rations with the animal until the dastardly deed. The Japs had to do a bayonet charge to break up the free for all. From then on the Dutch were always called 'dog scoffing bastards' by our Digger friends and great care was taken to keep the two factions apart as much as possible.

Work parties were marched down to the Docks every day for loading and off loading of cargoes of food supplies. This gave ample opportunity for plenty of 'nicking' now recognised as being an acceptable and legitimate business. The niceties of life had been dispensed with and everything evolved around the basic principle of survival. A man who was good at the smuggling game was looked up to as being a great guy. One thing he had to have was courage, because the Jap sentries took a very serious view of any of their particular party being caught, because the Japanese code of conduct dictated that the sentry himself could expect some punishment from his superiors. On one occasion the sentry caught one of the lads pinching a few bars of soap and decided there and then on the spot that he should eat some of the loot. Not very appetising. Water bottles had been doctored to contain about two inches of water on the top but the lower part had been sectioned off to contain most anything, by way of sugar, palm oil or even on one occasion spares for the wireless set which we afterwards found had been tied under the bamboo slats in the latrines. Every so often the Jap Authorities would do a swoop on the huts - the ensuing passing would have been a credit to Twickenham. One day during all this action I had a Gurka Kukri (knife) smartly passed into my hands by a panic stricken owner (not a Gurka). I had just time to drop it on the floor and stand on it. Good job the light was bad. When the search party had departed I advanced on this 'hero' with the kukri and he fled the scene at a fast rate of knots when I indicated that he would never be called Daddy.

This camp was to be the scene of a lot of brutal beat ups by one Korean known as 'The Storm Trooper', a big 6' brute of a man. It was to our everlasting regret that when we were shipped out of Singapore en route for Japan this sub-human was left behind. We knew that the tide of battle had turned against the I.J.A. and we were looking forward to a little bit of revenge, hence our reason for being prepared to take some stick just so long as some of these animals would be there for the taking when the time came. Make no mistake about it, the treatment which had been meted out to us enforced the principle of 'an eye for an eye - a tooth for a tooth'! Turning the other cheek was kid's stuff and not to be tolerated at any price.

Hell Ship

This departure from Keppel Harbour was not without misgivings when we were herded on a small utility type coastal vessel. About 400 souls were crammed below (decks) on the cargo decks, in fact the boat resembled an empty shell, lined on all sides with shelvings supposedly as sleeping berths. The only air intake was down the canvas funnels hanging over the open holds, and provided with bell like catchments, which were set up to face the 'pointed end' of the boat. This may have been okay when the boat was in motion on the open sea but of no consequence during the 24 hour wait in Keppel, and men were going down like flies and having to be hauled up the open metal stairway. There were two Vickers type machine guns in position on the bridge structure manned 24 hours a day by the Japanese troops and trained on the overcrowded P.O.W.'s. A small portion of the deck had been cleared, covered with metal flat sheets and the rice boilers or 'qualleys' built up on supporting concrete blocks. The cooks had to operate in this restricted area, feeding the open fires with logs of half green wood and attempt to feed the 400 prisoners. You can imagine the chaos when the occasional tropical storm hit us as we lurched our way across the Gulf of Siam before striking East into the China Sea, ostensibly on our way to Japan. Much as they would have liked, the machine gunners could not keep us down in the stinking fetid bowels of the boat. We considered it was better to die in the fresh air than just curl up and die down below. Along with two more chaps I had squatted on a jib overlooking the hold and there I was to stay for six days and nights, just coming down to relieve myself or to hand out my half mess tin for the usual pap rice and portion of hot boiled water. After six days sitting like a starling on the jib I felt surprisingly fit but had a worrying time when I saw the unconscious body of my brother being carried forward along with many, many more. It was hours before one of my mates informed me that Bill was okay in that he was alive but in a bad way with a malarial attack. The dead were just slung over the side with no prayers or fuss. Not many of us were very kindly disposed towards the Almighty during this period, so there was no point in adding hypocrisy to our list of vices like lying, thieving, or hating, all directed against our hosts. The very act of relieving oneself was a study in gymnastic ability. There were seven large boxes lashed along the side of the boat and situated just below the deck level. Each of these boxes had two of the centre boards knocked out and the trick was to gauge the shake, rattle or roll of the boat before clambering over the hand-rails and lowering into the boxes, feet straddled on the remaining floor of the box, and praying that the footrests were secure. This frightening ordeal was practically the only known cure for dysentery because having once been over the side there was a tendency to ignore the calls of nature. One wag had actually nicked a bit of white chalk from some source and written in bold letters 'NOT TO BE USED WHILE THE SHIP IS STOPPED' and although it was just a few inches from the nose of the temporary passenger it wasn't easy to laugh when hanging on for grim death and trying to fulfil your purpose.

Like everything else the boat was fuelled with logs, and many were the curses aimed at the Chinese crew when flying sparks settled amongst the overcrowded passengers. This indiscriminate fuelling was to save our very lives later on when an American submarine pack got amongst the convoy and wrought havoc on everything in sight. It had been noticed that the stokers always made the sparks fly at night and we afterwards found out that that had been a marker for the pursuing submarines who realised that this boat was a prison ship, therefore to be avoided.

One attack at night was a bit panicky until old sailor Ben Raven (Aussie, one time Merchant Navy and now Cook Sgt) assured us that when our boat was jumping up out of the water it was just the repercussion from torpedo strikes on other ships. I had a great view from my lofty perch but some of the bangs had me clinging on by the teeth. The attack lasted for most of the night, and the following day revealed that the survivors were one cargo boat limping in our wake and the Jap escort Cruiser. It was said afterwards that it was a deliberate policy to allow the cruiser to escape because of the realisation that we may have been tempted to take over the boat and thereby sign our death warrant. The reason for this was our close proximity to Saigon at the time and the known fact that there was a strong gathering of Jap air strength, who could have blown us out of the water without hours. So much for being wise after the event but at the time of the action emotion was the ruling factor and caution a fleeting expression.

In normal peace time in the Far East we called the Chinese 'slant eyed shirt destroying bastards (laundrymen)' but now they were our saviours, may the Holy Dragon bless them.

Time marches on, and so did the boat until one morning I ruffled my feathers, looked across the water and realised we were entering a river mouth about a mile wide and gradually decreasing in width. We were to travel up this river for a few miles constantly dodging the wrecks of previously sunk vessels. The long hazardous journey was over and had we but known was to be our last major move because by now the Americans were the masters of the Phillipines and closing in fast. On arrival at the Saigon Dock side we wobbled ashore on shaky knees and were bedded down in the large Nissen type storage buildings. The mere fact of their being empty indicated to us that all was not well for the I.J.A. and also an indication that Uncle Sam 'ruled the waves' in this area of conflict. Twin fuselage 'Lockheed Lightnings' were overflying every day, and although we only occupied the large 'Go-Downs' for a couple of days our presence was well recorded on aerial survey maps, which were shown to us a few months later. These planes were fitted with auxiliary fuel tanks which were jettisoned when their function was complete. The first sight of these aluminium tanks falling from the planes caused panic all round. They could be seen spinning over and over in the sunlight from about 30,000 feet and to we 'behind the times' mortals it could have been a flying bomb of some sort. All this buzzing by the Yanks gave us a great lift, and we had to be very careful not to appear too arrogant at this stage because by the same activity so the Japanese became extremely touchy and liable to lash out at the least excuse.

Our new camp was just up the road from the Docks and I suppose was in a vulnerable position, but having come so far and survived the so-called Death Railway there was a general feeling of immortality amongst the inmates.

I suppose some characters are remembered more than others and this camp had three such individuals. One Japanese Sgt known as 'Big Nat' was an ambling 6 footer, who had reputedly represented his country in the 1936 Olympic Games. He was an expert swimmer. He was quite an amiable man, who would shut his eyes to many so-called misdemeanours, but at the same time never tried to curb the enthusiasm of two Korean guards notoriously known as 'The Beard' and 'The Face'. These two sadists would draw an imagined wrong-doing out of mid-air and after a false accusation would proceed to punish the victim. 'The Face' was a baby faced juvenile, who hadn't the sense to see that the end was in sight and carried on kicking and bashing until the bitter end, but more of him later. 'The Beard' was a different kettle of fish and would have been a sinister man in 'Al Capone's' gang. There was an aura of evil around him and he was avoided at practically any cost. To be drafted on to his daily work party at any time was a black day indeed, because some poor soul was sure to be beaten up if it was only by way of exercise for this monster. All the outside work operating from this camp was 'risk' jobs, especially now when planes were homing in from the Phillipines and treating the Japanese Zeros with total disdain. The big 'Flying Fortresses' were doing the occasional high level bombing runs on the airfields, docks, etc. and amazingly, although the P.O.W.'s were working the clock round in these areas, there was not one casualty. (Come to think maybe there was a God.) Slit trenches were dotted here and there around the airfield and every gymnastic dive in was hilarious, in that the Korean guard gave the signal when we were supposed to take cover and this was usually the last moment when a stick of bombs were on their way. The guard always contrived to be nearest the trench before giving the signal to submerge into the deck, but it was debatable which was the safer, being dived on in rugby league style or taking his chance with flying debris. Although we loved these big 'birds' and showed it (Who loves ya, baby?) the Japanese and Koreans were quick to take retribution against any prisoner showing such enthusiasm. I was pointing out the incoming of some Lockheeds one day and the gesture was believed by the Korean goon to be a welcoming wave. First thing I know is the close proximity of hundreds of little lights or stars and then oblivion. I came round to the face slapping of one of my mates, who informed me that 'The Face' had hit me from behind with the rifle butt before diving for cover. As luck happened the bombs were dropped on the other side of the airfield so apart from a duck egg on the back of the head and a fair amount of blood, it had been decreed that I would live to hate another day. Another one for the King! And another black mark against 'The Face'.

During our coming and going to the various outside jobs there was often a face to face meeting with the Vichy French Community. It was very embarrassing from both sides, what with our Jap Happy loincloths and bare feet and their European white tropical attire, complete with pith helmet. At least we knew what side of the fence we were on and not just in limbo neither one thing or at the other. I think we pitied them and no doubt piled on the humiliation for them. The French community occupied the tree lined boulevards in the McPherson Road suburbs, and apart from coming and going to their place of business would more or less stay in their own area, so in a way they were as much prisoners as we.

'Le Guerre Fini!'

Unbeknown to most of us some of the P.O.W.'s had outside contacts and were being fed the news items albeit weeks behind the times, rather like saving the cake until the last. However, came the day when word spread like wildfire about some huge bomb having been dropped on the Japanese mainland. In fact, the Japs and Korean guards were going around with long faces and calling Roosevelt, Stalin and Churchill No. 10 which was their interpretation of their being 'bad men' or damme! damme! They were going around with a dazed look, muttering "Boom, Boom!" and not the way Basil Brush says it.

On the 15th August 1945 we were told to pack our meagre belongings and prepare for a trip up river and thence through the canal system to Pnom Phen. It was on the cards that a defence system was being set up and the intention that the 150,000 Japanese troops in the Saigon complex were going to continue the war even if there was an official cease fire. This would mean the end for any Allied prisoners, once they were of no further use. We were hustled down to the Docks, there to embark on rice barges and linked up three barges at a time to the motorised 'pom-poms'. A machine gun was mounted on each of the pom-poms and facing back to cover each of the barges in case anyone attempted to do a Johnny Weismuller.

The two day journey was uneventful except for the occasional shout of paddy field workers, something which sounded very much like "La Guerre Fini! La Guerre Fini!". That may be so, but there was no arguing with our slant eyed friends manning the machine guns, and there wasn't much point being dead even if you were right. On the evening of the second day the barges were tied up to the bank whilst the forward pom pom unhitched and pulled ahead until it disappeared out of sight round a bend in the canal. We could hear the 'Phut Phut' of the exhausts dying away into the distance. Some two hours later it returned and in the half light could be seen a Japanese officer in ceremonial dress and samurai sword round the waist. Now then could this be the big wipe out of some 100 or so prisoners or the ceremonial 'Hari Kari'? We dreaded one but welcomed the other. Neither was to be, but a rather respectable request that "all men yasumi". 'All men' were fairly hardened to any eventuality after 3½ years living the life of a coolie, but even so the uncertainty of the situation made a very fitful sleepless night for most.

There was a tense feeling of excitement running through the ranks of P.O.W.'s and all the murmured conversation centred round the same question. Was 'La Guerre Fini' according to the native information or was this just another cruel unfounded hope?

It was generally agreed that if the barges turned round facing back the way we had come there was every possibility that the war was indeed over, and not only that, but the certainty that the I.J.A. had accepted the ultimatum of downing arms rather than stand and fight after destroying all the evidence of ill treatment of thousands of Allied P.O.W.'s.

The suspense was still facing us the following morning when the strung out barges continued up stream but the uncertainty turned to jubilation when we entered a stretch of water of lake like proportion, and proceeded to do a wide circular sweep before coming back down the canal. At the same time it was noted that the machine gun crew adopted a more relaxed attitude and actually handed out a few cigarettes to those nearest. Although we had a two day journey up the canal and river the journey back was cut by half and we were within sight of the familiar Dock side by evening of the first day, before tying up to an old wharf. Some of the braver souls decided to go over the side for a swim, but I considered this a stupid risk after coming through all the terrors of the 3½ years of captivity. I decided that as of now I was going to tread very carefully and hope that I would once again see a plate of eggs/bacon, white bread and a pint of good old English beer.

No official word had been given of any cease fire, but the general relaxed demeanour of the guards gave us the hopeful clue that this was so. We stayed tied up to the old wharf the whole of that night but I don't think anyone slept.

Early next morning we glided the last half mile or so into the Docks proper, there to be greeted by one of our own officers with the fantastic news that the I.J.A. had, on orders from the Emperor himself, decided to down arms. The one condition being that certain weapons be retained for their own protection. So much for the S.E. Asia Co. Prosperity dream.

The march back to the camp was just a delirious dream with Vichy French and the native population pressing food, clothing and cigarettes into our eager hands. We were still under armed sentry protection and were to remain so until details had been thrashed out for our evacuation. Food which had been non-existent before now became plentiful, and the danger of over indulgence was a real risk, or at least we thought it was a risk. As a matter of fact, very few of us were able to eat much owing to stomach shrinkage over the $3^1/2$ years of starvation diet. The first day in camp was spent in sitting around, smoking our heads off and having a patriotic gathering round the flat pole where the Jap 'fried-egg' had been replaced with a home made Union Jack. This show of aggression had been watched by the impassive six man guard, who appeared to be too dazed to care. In the afternoon there was an overhead show of strength by R.A.F. planes flying very low and jiggling the wings in salute before dropping large cannisters of supplies. These supplies were dropped on the outskirts of the camp and there was a beeline run by the more fittest to get them into camp before the native population could get to them. The grand climax of the day's event came when three jungle clad figures strode into the camp and this was really the confirmation of something we couldn't grasp - FREEDOM! These three were like people from outer space to us and the big 6' 4" leader quickly asserted his authority by demanding the location of the Camp Commandant - one Suzuki (Capt) of his Imperial Highness Hirihoto.

At the time of their bursting into the camp, some of us were attempting to have a wash-down at the communal watering trough in the camp centre and I think the sight of British soldiers now emaciated beyond recognition would incense him into doing a rash deed. When one of our party offered to bring Suzuki he would have none of it but turned to one of his companions saying "Send one of those monkeys and tell him to be here in two minutes flat"! The 'monkeys' being the still armed sentries. Suzuki came round the building nearest the Jap guard house indicating that he had been close to his armed guard all along. The leader of the trio (afterwards named as being a Wing Cmmdr Campbell) made Capt Suzuki run the last few yards by reaching for his pistol holster. Suzuki stood to attention and was midway to a military salute when the Wing Cmmdr reached forward. grasped the broad belt around Suzuki's waist, undid the buckle, and pulled to one side so that three things happened at the same time: (1) the pull on one side made Suzuki spin like a top, (2) his pants fell down and (3) the belt plus sword was now firmly in the hands of the Wing Cmmdr. To crown the performance the Wing Cmmdr gave Suzuki a crack over his bare posterior with the still encased sword! Never was a samurai sword put to better use, and for this action the Wing Cmmdr was treated to a resounding cheer, but regretfully, we learned later on that he had been court martialled for ungentlemanly conduct. His intention was to humiliate Suzuki and the armed guard in front of prisoners who had been down-trodden, kicked around and humiliated for so long. His very act did more good than any man made tonic because the tension of the many years appeared to evaporate, and from that time on the armed guard were just 'part of the furniture' and totally ignored.

The main camp gate was lifted off the hinges and anyone wishing to go out of the camp precincts was at liberty to do so. This could have dire consequences because there was a clash of political parties known as the Viet Cong. and the Viet Minh. Somehow or other Japanese arms had come into their possession and there was quite a bit of activity around the City centre. Nevertheless we just continued to walk into this action zone knowing that both sides would treat us as neutrals provided we made no attempt to interfere. Some of the Vichy French invited us to their homes during this period of freedom but we weren't very keen because a feeling of mistrust prevailed, and our friendship was more directed to the native population who like ourselves, had taken the brunt of all the hard knocks, which more or less made us blood brothers. The invitation we did accept was to tour the brewery and stock rooms and a riotous old time was had by one and all! What else? Some do-good member of the military mission decided to provide us with a barrel of navy rum but our palate couldn't accept such nectar. The intention was good however, because a couple of our lads had bought a native concoction which was well laced with 'wood alcohol' and apparently it had sent him blind. The rum was very strong and had to be diluted but at least there was no danger of impairing sight, and taken in moderation was a good booster. Discipline, as such, was non-existent except in our own common sense to behave in a reasonable manner until such times as we could be evacuated, and this could only be carried out when planes became available from the Burma front. I personally think we had to wait until the pilots had finished celebrating the 'grand slam' over the Axis forces and now the Japanese! Who could blame them?

On the 1st September, 1945, one of the Allied members of the R.A.P.W.I. (Rehabilitation of Allied P.O.W.'s and Internees) came into the camp and gave the age old order of "Gather round, chaps!". He proceeded to lecture us on the folly of leaving the camp area but we weren't having any of his blarney but rather that he came to the point of his visit - "When do we go home?". He explained that owing to the shortage of aircraft we could only be uplifted in teams of 20 at a trip as the 'Dakotas' would be fully loaded at this number even with all seating and accoutrements stripped. We were requested to make up our own teams of 20 and designate one of each team as leader so that his name could go into the hat to be drawn out in order of priority 'lifts'! Even at this stage I was cautious and agreed with my brother to be in separate teams so as to ascertain the greater chance of at least one of us getting home safely. None of us had ever flown before and the sight of these old 'Dakotas' didn't exactly exude confidence. In fact, the combination of old, battered planes and young baby faced pilots didn't appear too good to us. All our fears were unfounded because they were the best, with control second to none. The hat draw made me the fourth lift for my team and the airlift would probably commence the following day so it was up to ourselves to keep together in our teams, as failure to be there would put us to the end of the queue and a possible lynching by the other team members! It was the ruling later adopted for Union policy of 'one out, all out'. My brother was unlucky on this occasion as this team were the 24th lift and was later to mean being relegated to the second boat out of Rangoon, and my being home three weeks before him.

Lift Off!

The lift off from Saigon Airport was a bit of a frightener for my team as the old flappy winged Dakota rumbled down the pock-marked runway while we sat on the floor of the empty shell of a fuselage, head between knees, and I, for one, praying to a God I had doubted even existed. We made it with inches to spare and the flight path took us over our old camp site, up into the blue sky. This was the first time for all my years of captivity that I really felt clean and I did a mental 'wet-dog' shake to heighten the illusion of complete severance. Excitement was running high, and one or two of the lads were sick but quickly recovered before touching down at Bangkok for refuel and to receive our first issue of Red Cross cigarettes, chocolate and concentrated survival vitamins in case of accidents. About an hour sitting under the shade of the wings of the aircraft while the re-fuelling and maintenance teams buzzed around and having to put up with a chorus of "Why are we waiting", and earnest pleas that the elastic take off mechanism have a thorough overall. A new crew had now taken over from here, on to Rangoon and we were soon airborne and heading N.E. until we actually followed 'our railway' where so many of our comrades had died. The pilot came down so that we could look out of the side windows and follow the snake like track through the jungle with here and there a good view of the many bridges which spanned the gulleys or ravines. I think the sight of this killer track upset a few of our party and for myself, I thought I was just dreaming and any moment would wake up hacking and digging my way along side the rail embankment. It was with relief that the railway faded away to our rear and the jungle gave way to an expanse of water, the Gulf of Martaban in fact, and then part of the Irrawaddy before touching down on a battered runway of Rangoon Airfield, to be whisked away in a waiting fleet of ambulances, to the big hospital. This was to be the first time that any attempt be made to get particulars of number, rank, name, religion etc. etc. So that our next of kin could be informed. None of us were even sure that we had any next of kin, and by the same token my Father must have been worried by the reporting of myself but not his favourite son, who was still in Saigon awaiting an air lift. I tried to explain this omission to the clerk but although he was very sympathetic he maintained that there was nothing he could do. No 'body' to report.

Rangoon, Edwina And Bill Slim

The emphasis was now on a speedy pass through of ex-P.O.W.'s, to allow for the next intake, so provided you had two arms, two legs etc. the verdict of 'fit to travel' was stamped on our temporary statistic cards. The Transit camp was a huge tented lay-out complete with Naafi facilities and beer so our two days and nights in residence was one long party and entertainment. The E.N.S.A. people were vastly out-numbered by our own team of singers, dancers, comedians and jugglers who quickly took over the stage, and I have a very distinct memory of one, McFadgian of the Gordons, trying to fly from the marquee cross beam with the aid of a ground sheet round the shoulders, and declaring to all and sundry that he was 'Dracula' He was lucky to escape with a broken ankle but at least he learnt one fact of life - he couldn't fly!

Two distinguished visitors saw us in these two days, Lady Mountbatten (who really was a lady) and General Bill Slim. They were distinguished to us, not because of their high office but because both had the common touch and feet planted firmly on the ground.

Lady Edwina gave us a short talk on the stupidity of going down the town 'looking for red flannel' and that it was her dearest wish that we reach home safely and, after the long sea voyage, in better health. She also pointed out that we were eligible to have a six month's convalescence in Australia if we wished. There didn't appear to be many volunteers except for a few of the lads who had received 'Dear John' letters from the build up of mail which had now been distributed. Some took it hard and attempted to hit the bottle but some there were who took it in their stride and adopted the sensible attitude of 'good riddance'! Some of these marriages had been spur of the moment tie-ups and due, no doubt, to the emotional times of eat, drink and be merry. The left at home wives couldn't always be blamed but rather the Army system prevailing just prior to the war, which decreed a man could be sent to a foreign station for many years. For instance, most Regulars joined the services for 7 years with the Colours and 5 years on Reserve so that in the event of hostilities breaking out the servicemen could finish up doing 12 years with the Colours. Some of my comrades in the Manchester Regt had been posted to the West Indies in 1934 for a period of 2 years, then a quick return in 1936 for a 12 hour leave on the quay side at Portsmouth to meet their families who had been transported down from Manchester with a lot of bally-ho.

Trouble had broken out in the Middle East and their presence was required in the Western Desert and 12 hours was the only break for many years. From the Middle East to Singapore in 1938 and of course, the outbreak of the war meant they were well and truly encased in the system. Where some had enlisted for 7 and 5 years, they did, in fact, do anything up to 16 years with the colours and 'no pension' to show for it, because 21 years was the absolute minimum service for pension. How was it possible for marriages to stand up under this sort of separation? Ridiculous!

Homeward Bound

We sailed out of Rangoon in September 1945 in a Dutch Liner (Bousenvain) and after our recent mode of existence the present luxury was overwhelming, even though most of us bedded down on the open deck. The boat was fully stocked with everything imaginable, even to the beer bar, where a ration of two pints per man, per day, was the allocation. No heed being taken of the fact that some men were teetotal and their beer chits being handed over to their mates, there was a 'Nellie Dean' chorus every night from various parts of the boat.

Some of the upper crust officers attempted to take over the lush 1st Class lounges and put up notices regarding these emporiums being out of bounds to 'other ranks'. The notices promptly finished up in the Indian Ocean and some of the protesting officers nearly finished up in the same place. They had the Sandhurst outlook that the world was peopled by two classes - 'Gentlemen' and 'Other Ranks'. How wrong they were and how quickly they learnt when this illusion was brought to their notice. Our 'going through the mill' experiences had already sorted out the 'gentlemen' from the others, and shoulder 'pips' counted as nothing to us. There was an absolute refusal to accept discipline in the old Army sense. Consultation - yes, direct ordering - no chance! Boys had matured into men, and common sense was the deciding factor in what, and what not to do for our own welfare. This attitude was to prevail during the whole of the journey and I never at any time saw any attempt to take advantage of the situation and before we had been at sea a few days the officers were fraternising with the lower ranks and addressing them as Mr. - how's that for a mutual understanding and a respect of human rights? Incidentally, there were cinema shows and we first beheld Frank Sinatra on the silver screen as well as seeing Bing (the old groaner) singing 'White Christmas'.

Our entrance into Ceylon was something we shall never forget. There were hundreds of boats massed, Warships, Troopers, Destroyers, Submarines, leaving a lane down which we sailed to a crescendo of howling sirens, big hooters and cheers from the crews and troops on the Trooper decks. One would have thought we were conquering heroes instead of returning ex P.O.W.'s. A very humbling experience but one which said 'Welcome home, lads!'. This should have been the naval Task Force all ready for taking over by force from the Japanese in Singapore and only the dropping of the Atom bomb curtailed this operation. I've often thought that had this task force been a month earlier there would have been a great uplift of prestige in that area and but for the loss of life would have been a booster for the British armed forces. We know we gave the Japanese the grand slam in Burma, but seeing is believing to the residents of Singapore.

Our stay in Ceylon was only a matter of hours to do a pick up of military staff, who boarded ship with the same 'officer-other ranks' dogma but a few days later were good humouredly indoctrinated into the ways of these strange men from the Jap prison camps. Mind you, the actual ship's crew were obeyed at all times. They knew their jobs and if we were in the way they told us so. Fair enough. Most of our voyage was taken up with 'Tombola' or 'Crown and Anchor', the age long unwritten law coming into effect here, where only a ship's crew member being allowed to run the 'Crown and Anchor' school.

Our next call was Port Tewfik where we were kitted out with military battle dress and side hats. Each man had a 'batman' of one of Rommel's Afrika Corps to carry the kit bag around the big stores compounds to draw the various items after the usual too big, too small trial fittings. Never having fought against the Germans we found it hard to imagine that these Afrika Corps men were the ex-enemy and we were lashing the fags out to them much to the annoyance of the 'Red Caps' guards. My old mate Harry (sometimes John) Proctor handed a packet of fags to his particular helper only to see the guard snatch them off him again. Harry (sometimes John) was incensed and all of his 5' 4" threatened to throw all 6' of the guard into the 'drink' if he didn't return them to the P.O.W. pretty damn quick The re-action took the guard by surprise who backed down from this little fury and promptly returned them. Such were our ways of camaraderie between one ex-P.O.W. to one still in the bag.

'Scouse Welcome'

The rest of the voyage home was just one holiday cruise until we eventually docked in Liverpool on October 10th, 1945 (I had then been in the Far East for 7¹/₂ years). The fog was so intense that we had ghosted up to the quay-side - before being aware of any movement. Then the air exploded with sirens, hooters, voices - the lot. The Ship's Tannoy system instructed that embarkation would begin in one hour and every man to have his personal belongings ready for lift and move out, or, as the voice commanded 'prepare to pick up your parrots and monkeys'! There was a fleet of buses ready to whip us away to a local transit camp at Maghull but the kind hearted Scousers slowed down the proceedings by invading the buses and going wild with joy.

The next two days was a whirlwind of activity with the authorities pulling out all the stops to get this undisciplined rabble off their hands. This was the reference made by a Coy. Sgt. Major with a Barrack Square mentality and who had decided that we fall in on a 'right marker', 'eyes right' etc. etc. We decided we wouldn't, and that was that! I think he retreated behind one of the utility buildings and cut his throat. In spite of this little set back we were very quickly fixed up with rail warrants and an advance of £10 per man to meet travelling expenses. I had this over-riding impulse to set off on foot so as not to miss any of this green and pleasant land which had just been a dream for so many years. My little friend John (sometimes Harry) Proctor talked me out of this mad notion and so we travelled home together by train, back to bonny Cumberland, the hills, rivers, the pubs and fish shops!

The Completed Circle

My home village of Cleator was bedecked with bunting and 'Welcome' signs from every window. The only fly in the ointment being the absence of my Brother, Bill, who had been held up awaiting shipment from Rangoon and then having a further hold up in the Suez - due to one of the home coming 'Troopers' being burnt out and blocking the water way for some considerable time. I was to be home for ten days before Bill turned up and every day I was asked if I was covering up the possibility that he wasn't coming home at all. I was all confused at the time and not sure about anything. For instance, try and imagine the commonly accepted fact that on awakening each day it would be known whether it to be Monday, Tuesday, or whatever. I had to go buy a news-paper for this information because over the years of captivity this natu-ral thinking mechanism had been shattered. It was many months before this civilised mode of thinking became part of me. Whenever I hear the expression "He doesn't know what day it is"! I shiver a little.

During this rehabilitation period I was to meet the lady who later became my wife. She was a war widow with one daughter (Valerie Jane) and both Ruby and daughter, Valerie, were a great source of strength to me during a very trying period of hospitalisation. I was in and out of hospital for nearly three years before I was sorted out after every medical avenue in the book had been explored from psychiatric mumbo jumbo to basic prods, 'Lumbar punches' and diets. I'll be for-ever thankful to a 'baby' doctor who put his talented finger right on the bottom and prescribed the appropriate treatment for a very virulent tropical bug which had been lying dormant and drawing on my life's blood. I was extremely sorry later on for making cynical remarks to this young chap when he first took me under his care but throughout it all he remained unruffled and it was a shame faced I who thanked him by apologising.

I had been through my Singapore battles to Kwai and for me the war should be over but old battles still persist in the still of the night.

Epilogue

Although most of long days and months of captivity were taken up with dreaming and talking about revenge for the inhuman behaviour of most of the Jap camp administrators, when it came to the actual crunch I very much doubt that the 'eye for an eye' dogma could have been physically carried out by most of us. We were heartily sick of violence. Not so soft centred were a bunch of Australians who hunted down and cornered one of our tormentors. 'The Face' was caught trying to hide away in the Chinese quarter of Cholon (Saigon) and I had to witness the most cold blooded act of revenge by these ten executioners. The victim was stood up within a perimeter formed by the Aussies and systematically punched to death. It was a slow death and even after death he was stamped into the ground until he was just pulp. The hunt was then on for his friend - 'The Beard', but this animal managed to cover his tracks.

My reaction to the witnessing of this act of revenge was one of disgust but at the same time gave me hope for the future and the realisation, that perhaps there was still a spark of compassion and feeling for my fellow-men. This civilised feeling I thought had been left behind in the hell camps along the banks of the Kwai.